TIMES OF THE SIGNS

George Curle

*"Do return, O Lord; How long
will it be?"* Psalm 90:13

*"Those who have insight
will understand."* Dan. 12:10

New Wine Press

Typesetting and layout © 1988 New Wine Press

New Wine Press
P.O.Box 17
Chichester PO20 6RY
England

ISBN 0 947852 239

To my wife
CORAL

I dedicate this book. Her love to the Lord, her continuous exhortation and encouragement to the truth of the Lord's return, her loyalty to me during the lean years and through the straight places have been these forty-two years, and remain, a value *"far above rubies. The heart of her husband doth safely trust in her.... she will do him good and not evil all the days of her life."*

(Proverbs 31)

"SEARCH THE SCRIPTURES"

"It is the glory of God to CONCEAL a matter; to SEARCH out a matter is the glory of Kings." (Proverbs 25:2)

"Concerning this salvation, the prophets who spoke of the grace that was to come to you SEARCHED INTENTLY and with the greatest care, trying to find out the TIME and CIRCUMSTANCES to which the Spirit of Christ in them was pointing when He PREDICTED the sufferings of Christ, and the glories that would follow..." (1 Peter 1:10-12)

....*"Even angels long to LOOK into these things".* (1 Peter 1:12)

"If you SEARCH for it as for hidden treasure, then you will understand...and find the knowledge of God." (Proverbs 2:4)

"So I turned my mind to understand, to investigate and to SEARCH out....the scheme of things." (Ecclesiastes 7:25)

"They SEARCHED the scriptures daily to see if these things were so." (Acts 17:11)

"From now on I will tell you of NEW things, of HIDDEN things unknown to you.... you have not heard of them before today. So you cannot say, 'Yes I knew them'. You have neither heard nor understood." (Isaiah 48:6-8).

"Let a man so account of us, as.... stewards of the MYSTERIES of God." (1 Corinthians 4:1 AV)

"The ways of the Almighty I will not CONCEAL." (Job 27:11)

ACKNOWLEDGMENTS

DR. EDWIN R. THIELE for establishing an absolute date in Old Testament Chronology in his book "The Mysterious Numbers of the Hebrew Kings.

DR. HAROLD W. HOEHNER for establishing an absolute date in New Testament Chronology in his book "Chronological Aspects of the Life of Christ."

MISS LEILA 'TWINK' CORBAN. I will be ever grateful to this remarkable lady, who made time during her very busy schedule to proof-read and give valuable critical appraisal on various aspects of the text.

MRS. SUE CURLE, my daughter-in-law, who on the eve of her overseas departure, graciously found time to type urgently required additional chapters.

MR. LYALL GREEN who so generously allowed the use of the latest technological equipment to speed up the preparation of this book.

MRS. PATRICIA GRYLLS for her tireless patience and endless enthusiasm in typing the manuscript.

THE LATE MR. LES LAWRY, my bible class leader in Nelson. When I was only fifteen, he thoroughly explained to me the 'Seventy' Weeks' of Daniel - the chronological vertebrate of prophecy, thus instilling in me a lifetime interest in the prophetic scriptures.

FOREWORD

Biographers acknowledge that the great seventeenth century mathematician and physicist, Sir Isaac Newton, spent almost as much time in a futile attempt to reconcile the dates of secular history with the Bible, as he spent doing physics. Mr. George Curle, himself an ingenuous synthesizer of the works of others, has succeeded in doing that which Sir Isaac could not.

One can not say with certainty what the full historical implications of this work might be, but Mr. Curle has here a unique contribution to an already prolific body of commentary on the apocalyptic age in which we live.

Times of the Signs is an examination of the time cycles of human history in the light of God's plan of redemption. It was in "the fullness of time" that Christ was born of a virgin (Gal. 4:4), and the final countdown of God's plan is also interwoven with biblical chronology, for it is in "the dispensation of the fulness of times". (Eph. 1:10) that all history will culminate in the return of Messiah to claim the right to David's throne as King of Kings.

While it is true that no man knows the exact day or hour, Christ did make it clear that God's children should be aware of the general context of the events leading up to the day of his return. When these things do begin to come to pass, we are to keep looking up, for our redemption "draweth nigh".

Surely Mr. Curle has clearly demonstrated that the return of our Lord is indeed near.

Dr. Kenneth F. McKinley, ThD., Professor of Bible and Archaeology, LeTourneau College, Longview, Tx.
Mr. A.D. Sanders, M.S., M. Div., S.T.M., Associate Professor of Physics and Astronomy.

PREFACE

This book on prophecy, containing much that is entirely new, demonstrates that there is a complete, harmonious interlocking pattern on the 'revealed years' from Genesis to Revelation. It also shows how approximately twenty Bible bearings all converge into a single year, well within the anticipated lifetime of most readers.

It does not set dates for the Rapture of the church or the Return of Christ - but gives the time frame, in years, for the last seven years of man's government of planet earth; after this there is a brief period that no-one can calculate prior to Christ's return (see Appendix four). You will no doubt be shocked, rocked and rotated as the implications of the factual material presented is absorbed. This world of evil, violence, child molesters, gang rapists, robbery, constant wars, Aids, terrorists is about to come to a sudden end! God has decreed a decisive, climatic moment when in Jesus Christ He will seize the reigns of world affairs, bring wickedness to a head for judgment, and establish righteousness on the earth.

As Josh McDowell says "The optimism portrayed by the prophets amaze me. The Bible clearly teaches that God is in control. There is hope. The world is racing towards a climax......

It will be Christ's dynamic return to earth to set up a thousand year reign of peace. Looking at the world situation and knowing that God is in control I am thankful to be alive today. What an opportunity - in a time of frustration, pessimisim and fear - to trust God to use His children in other people's lives; to be a ray of hope, a source of optimisim, an instrument to share Christ's love and forgiveness with others." (Prophecy Fact or Fiction p.p.4-5).

There is almost total ignorance world wide of the facts presented in this book. Christ predicted, *"As it was in the days of Noah, so will it be at the coming of the Son of Man....for they KNEW NOTHING about what would happen until the flood came and took them all away."* (Matthew 24:37-39).

Even among otherwise well informed Christians there is almost a black-out when it comes to knowledge of the end times - many are eschatologically illiterate. Even Job was baffled by this - *"wherefore since from the Almighty times are not hid, have His knowing ones no vision of His days?"* (Job 24:1 KJV).

This is a non-technical book addressed to the general reader. It was not written for mathematicians or theologians (except Prologue and Appendix Four). Its simple calculations are just time spans between certain historic events but its conclusions involve world shattering events, shortly to take place, affecting Christian and Non-Christian alike. It will become more and more obvious as one reads with an open and enquiring mind, that all our life plans will soon be dramatically disrupted for better or worse; also for most, their life expectancy will be drastically reduced.

Jesus said:- *"Be careful, or.... that day will close on you unexpectedly like a trap, for it will come upon all those who live on the face of the whole earth.... Pray that you may be able to escape all that is about to happen."* (Luke 21:34-36).

At present there is a plethora of books being published giving specific dates for the Rapture of the Church. This author strongly disassociates himself with any writer who tries to set dates for the Rapture or Second Advent, even within the parameter of one year.

If one could guess the exact date of the Rapture the Lord would alter it, just to prevent that person from boasting for all eternity.

CONTENTS

PROLOGUE

The Answers to three anticipated questions about this Book mainly for Theological Readers

1. Jesus said five times *"nobody knows the DAY nor the HOUR"*. How come you know?
2. Haven't others tried to give dates for the END of the age and failed?
3. Jesus said that the gospel of the kingdom has to be preached in the whole world before the END can come. As the Church is a long way from preaching the gospel to ALL the world surely the END cannot be in sight yet?

Informed Christians on prophecy have a real chronophobia about the end times, i.e. they have a fear of any teaching that issues in the fixing of a date - even getting as specific as one year. This phobia is deep-seated, understandable, and well founded, and is based largely on the above questions.

Let us deal with the most important question first, number one:- Five times Jesus said in Matthew 24 & 25 *"No-one knows the DAY nor the HOUR."* How come you know? The answer is simple - "I don't!" But let's look at the words of Jesus in the light of their context. Matthew 24 up to and including verse 30, describes the seven year period known as Daniel's 70th Week (Appendix 2). Then there is a PARENTHESIS, an interval, when signs and parables are given, then the message takes up again in verse 31 of Chapter 25. It is to this INDETERMINATE

11

time between the END of the seven years of tribulation, and the SECOND ADVENT that the warning *"No-one knows the day nor the hour"* applies. Five times the warning is given (Matthew 24:36, 42, 44, 50;25:13) and *all* are within the parameters of that period that no man can ever calculate i.e. *"Immediately after the tribulation of those days* (Matthew 24:29) *until "when the Son of Man shall come in His glory"* (Matthew 25:31) (see Diagram 1). For a fuller discussion of the matter see Sir Robert Anderson's classic "The Coming Prince" especially the latter half of his chapter on the 'Patmos Visions' (pages 182-187 in the 13th Edition (Appendix 4) and Chapter eight of his book 'Forgotten Truths'. See also interval in Zechariah 14:2 between Zechariah 13:8-9 and Zechariah 14:4 (see Dia 2).

QUESTION 2 "Doesn't the failure of others in the past to determine the END TIME preclude more attempts?

Well, men have formerly made big mistakes in their calculations respecting astronomy. Let me mention some of their failures concerning the distance of the sun. Copernicus said the sun was 4 millions of miles from the earth; the great Kepler said 13 Million; Sir Isaac Newton - 28 million. Ultimately, a proper method was discovered of working out the distance as approximately 92 million. Having obtained one method which was true, they soon found five others. Did astronomers cease their investigations because other men had failed? On the contrary, they profited by the failure of their predecessors.

The Wright brothers would never have become airborne if they had been discouraged by failures of the past - and so it is in every advancing field of science and discovery.

ONE BEARING NAVIGATORS

To my knowledge every prophetic writer of the past in this field has based his date on only ONE bearing - and no navigator can determine his position without

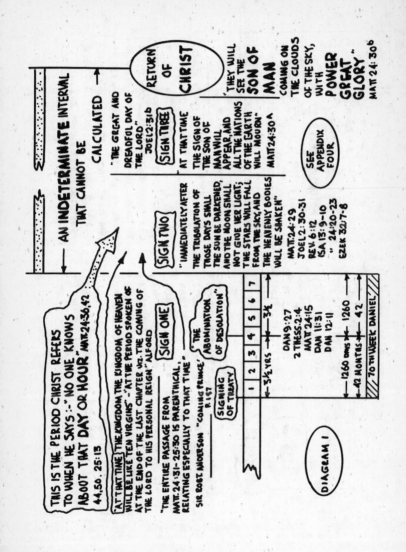

THIS IS THE PERIOD CHRIST REFERS TO WHEN HE SAYS:- "NO ONE KNOWS ABOUT THAT DAY OR HOUR" MAT.24:36,42 44,50. 25:13

AN INDETERMINATE INTERVAL THAT CANNOT BE CALCULATED

"AT THAT TIME THE KINGDOM THE KINGDOM OF HEAVEN WILL BE LIKE TEN VIRGINS" - "AT THE PERIOD SPOKEN OF AT THE END OF THE LAST CHAPTER VIZ. THE COMING OF THE LORD TO HIS PERSONAL REIGN" ALFORD

"THE ENTIRE PASSAGE FROM MATT. 24:31- 25:30 IS PARENTHICAL, RELATING ESPECIALLY TO THAT TIME" SIR ROBT. ANDERSON "COMING PRINCE" P. 157

RETURN OF CHRIST

"THE GREAT AND DREADFUL DAY OF THE LORD" JOEL 2:31b

SIGN THREE

AT THAT TIME THE SIGN OF THE SON OF MAN WILL APPEAR, AND ALL THE NATIONS OF THE EARTH WILL MOURN" MATT.24:30A

SEE APPENDIX FOUR

"THEY WILL SEE THE SON OF MAN COMING ON THE CLOUDS OF THE SKY, WITH POWER GREAT GLORY." MAT 24: 30b

SIGN TWO

"IMMEDIATELY AFTER THE TRIBULATION OF THOSE DAYS SHALL THE SUN BE DARKENED, AND THE MOON SHALL NOT GIVE HER LIGHT, THE STARS WILL FALL FROM THE SKY, AND THE HEAVENLY BODIES WILL BE SHAKEN"

MAT.24:29
JOEL 2:30-31
REV. 6:12
ISA 13: 9-10
" 24:20-23
EZEK 32:7-8

SIGN ONE

"THE ABOMINATION OF DESOLATION"

| 1 | 2 | 3 | 4 | 5 | 6 | 7 |

5½ YRS ———— 3½

DAN 9:27
2 THESS.2:4.
MAT.24:15
DAN 11:31
DAN 12:11

1260 DAYS ———— 1260
42 MONTHS ———— 42

SIGNING OF TREATY

70TH WEEK DANIEL

DIAGRAM I

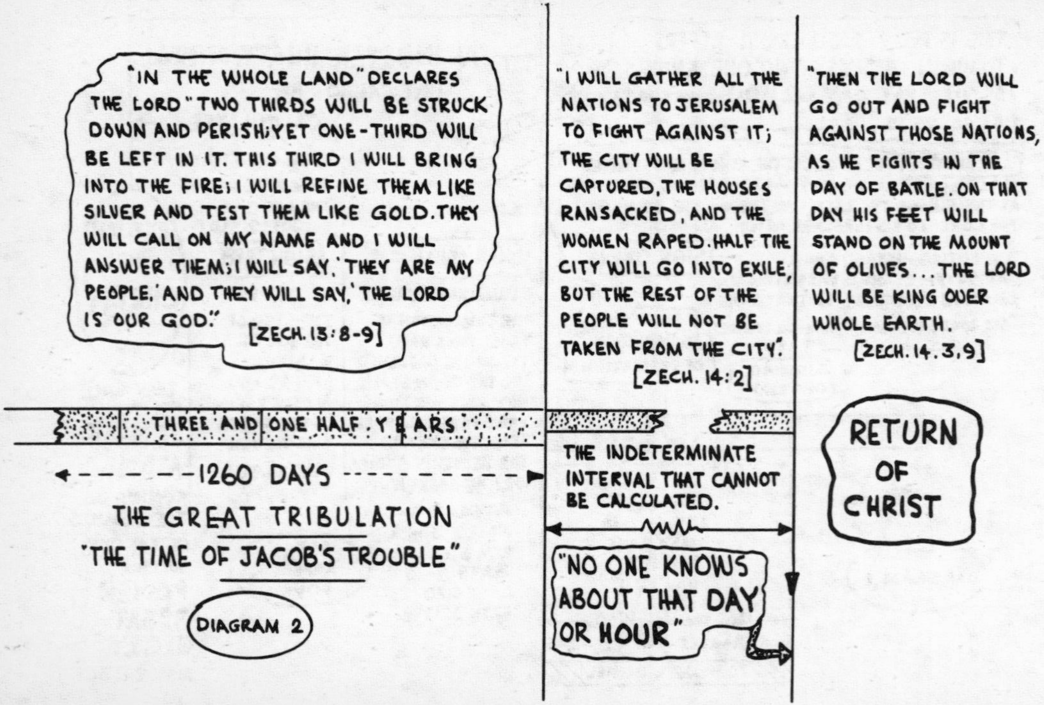

"IN THE WHOLE LAND" DECLARES THE LORD "TWO THIRDS WILL BE STRUCK DOWN AND PERISH;YET ONE-THIRD WILL BE LEFT IN IT. THIS THIRD I WILL BRING INTO THE FIRE; I WILL REFINE THEM LIKE SILVER AND TEST THEM LIKE GOLD.THEY WILL CALL ON MY NAME AND I WILL ANSWER THEM;I WILL SAY,'THEY ARE MY PEOPLE,'AND THEY WILL SAY,'THE LORD IS OUR GOD."

[ZECH.13:8-9]

" I WILL GATHER ALL THE NATIONS TO JERUSALEM TO FIGHT AGAINST IT; THE CITY WILL BE CAPTURED,THE HOUSES RANSACKED, AND THE WOMEN RAPED. HALF THE CITY WILL GO INTO EXILE, BUT THE REST OF THE PEOPLE WILL NOT BE TAKEN FROM THE CITY."

[ZECH. 14:2]

"THEN THE LORD WILL GO OUT AND FIGHT AGAINST THOSE NATIONS, AS WE FIGHTS IN THE DAY OF BATTLE . ON THAT DAY HIS FEET WILL STAND ON THE MOUNT OF OLIVES . . . THE LORD WILL BE KING OVER WHOLE EARTH.

[ZECH.14.3,9]

····· THREE AND ONE HALF · YEARS ···

------1260 DAYS------

THE GREAT TRIBULATION

"THE TIME OF JACOB'S TROUBLE "

THE INDETERMINATE INTERVAL THAT CANNOT BE CALCULATED.
~~~

"NO ONE KNOWS ABOUT THAT DAY OR HOUR"

RETURN OF CHRIST

DIAGRAM 2

14

another cross-bearing. Rev M. Baxter published a book in 1886 entitled "LOUIS NAPOLEON - DESTINED MONARCH OF THE WORLD." It was based on *one* bearing, and that bearing - historically worthless! On page 28 he plots 2520 years from 651 BC and comes correctly to the year 1870 AD. But what happened in 651 BC of prophetic significance? Nothing, absolutely nothing at all! Consulting several encyclopaedias of dates I have been unable to find one event secular or religious that occurred in 651 BC.

William Miller, founder of the Seventh Day Adventist Movement, was another *one* bearing navigator. In Daniel 8:14 a time period of 2300 days is mentioned. This apparently began on September 6, 171 BC. Miller made the days stand for years, and arrived at the date October 22, AD 1884 for the return of Christ.

Another *one* bearing navigator was Oswald J. Smith who in 1926 published his book "Is the Anti-Christ at Hand?" Using the wrong date for the fall of Jerusalem, 588 BC instead of 586 BC, he plotted 2520 years, and came up with the year 1933 for the end of the times of the Gentiles. He said "If our chronology is correct it means that all these things, including the great tribulation, the revival of the Roman Empire, the reign of Anti-Christ, and the battle of Armageddon must take place before the year 1933." (Quoted from 'The Coming Antichrist' by Walter K. Price p.39).

I could show you many more ONE bearing navigators from Augustine on, who have brought the marvellous study of Chronophecy (Chronological Prophecy) into disrepute. I know of no other work in this area of study that uses even TWO bearings that converge into a single year. In this book, the Lord, in His marvellous grace, has revealed to me many bearings from the Bible and history that cross, converge, connect and coincide with 2005 AD! All these bearings are based on historically accurate dates, and mathematically correct calculations.

Why did all these prophetic writers in the past fail?

Apart from their flimsy one bearing calculations why

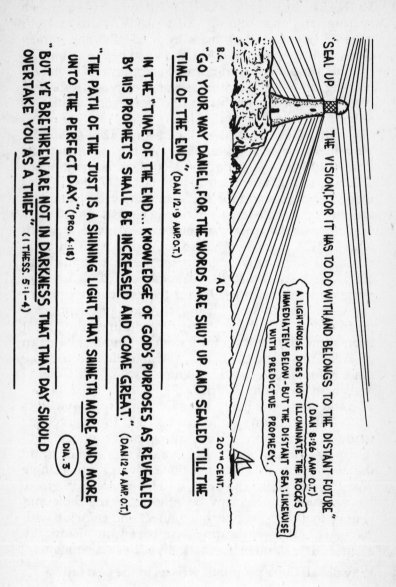

"SEAL UP THE VISION, FOR IT HAS TO DO WITH, AND BELONGS TO THE DISTANT FUTURE"
(DAN 8:26 AMP O.T.)

A LIGHTHOUSE DOES NOT ILLUMINATE THE ROCKS IMMEDIATELY BELOW — BUT THE DISTANT SEA; LIKEWISE WITH PREDICTIVE PROPHECY.

B.C.   A.D.   20TH CENT.

"GO YOUR WAY DANIEL, FOR THE WORDS ARE SHUT UP AND SEALED TILL THE TIME OF THE END" (DAN 12:9 AMP O.T.)

IN THE "TIME OF THE END ... KNOWLEDGE OF GOD'S PURPOSES AS REVEALED BY HIS PROPHETS SHALL BE INCREASED AND COME GREAT". (DAN 12:4 AMP. O.T.)

"THE PATH OF THE JUST IS A SHINING LIGHT, THAT SHINETH MORE AND MORE UNTO THE PERFECT DAY." (PRO. 4:18)

"BUT YE BRETHREN, ARE NOT IN DARKNESS THAT THAT DAY SHOULD OVERTAKE YOU AS A THIEF". (1 THESS. 5:1-4)

DIA. 3

16

did all these men fail and flounder in the dark where the end time was concerned? No doubt they were intelligent, earnest, sincere Christians - but their calculations vary from 650 AD (Augustine) to 1933 AD (Smith). Why did they not succeed?

The answer is simple. It just was not God's TIME to reveal the NEARNESS of His return. When the disciples asked the Lord, *"Lord, are you at this time going to restore the Kingdom to Israel?"* He wisely said to them: *"It is not FOR YOU to know the TIMES or the DATES"*. If Jesus had said "My feet won't touch this Mount of Olives for over 1900 years" it would have paralysed their faith, killed their hopes, blighted their joy and immobilised their plans for world evangelism.

How different is the position today as prophecy's beam comes more and more into focus. A lighthouse does not illuminate the rocks immediately below, but casts its light on the distant sea. As we read in Daniel *"In the time of the end, knowledge of God's purposes as revealed by the prophets shall be INCREASED and come GREAT."* (Daniel 12:4 Amp. Bible) (Diagram 3).

Paul Lee Tan in his excellent book "The Interpretation of Prophecy" says on page 116 "...since illumination will concern even 'things to COME' (John 16:13) we may EXPECT THAT AS THE CHURCH AGE DRAWS TO A CLOSE, AND MORE PROHETIC EVENTS ARE ABOUT TO TRANSPIRE, THE HOLY SPIRIT WILL GRANT MORE ILLUMINATION RELATIVE TO THE REFINEMENTS of prophecy. It seems as if God has allowed other doctrinal issues to be thrashed out in church history before fully opening up the study of prophecy to the church at the end of the age. The phenomenal growth of interest in the study of prophecy within the last century or so is significant. This may partially explain why the doctrine of the pretribulational rapture - the logical capstone of the entire eschatological structure - is now being emphasised by a significant portion of the Church." (Emphasis Mine)

Christ tells us we may know the NEARNESS

(Matthew 24:33) but not the EXACTNESS of His second coming (Matthew 24:36). He warns that all the fast moving, climactic end time events will be witnessed by the span of one generation who will be alive at the time. (Matthew 24:34-36).

He rebuked the Pharisees and Sadducees *"You know how to interpret the appearance of the sky, but you cannot interpret the signs of the times."* (Matthew 16:3). They knew more about meteorology, than they did about eschatology (the study of the last things).

Daniel *"understood from the books"* (Daniel 9:2) in his studies in Jeremiah 25:11-12, 29:10 that Jerusalem would shortly see the end of its desolations. He did not know the month or the week, or the day, or the hour - but he did learn *"the number of the years"* (Daniel 9:2) when it would come to pass.

There were wise men at Christ's first coming, who although they knew not *"the day nor the hour"* of His birth, were sufficiently informed as to the 'times and seasons' to be able to give Him a royal welcome. How much more should we be ready for His second coming *"in power and great glory"*. (Matthew 24:30 AV).

Young tender seedlings are kept in the DARK, and are only slowly and progressively exposed to more sunlight. Just as the ozone hole is enlarging at present, allowing more and more intense rays to reach this earth; so God is unsealing more and more prophetic light. May the increasing knowledge of His nearness warm our hearts, lift our hopes, increase our joy and mobilise us into earnest, effective evangelism.

QUESTION NO.3

Jesus said *"this gospel of the Kingdom will be preached in the whole world as a testimony to all nations, and then the END will come."* (Matthew 24:14).

As the church has not preached the gospel to all the world by a long way, the end cannot be in sight yet - so the objection is stated. Well, the gospel of the Kingdom is NOT the gospel of the grace of God. In Matthew 10:7

the twelve disciples were commanded to preach *"The Kingdom of Heaven is NEAR."* That this was not the gospel of the grace of God (i.e. the death, burial and resurrection of Christ) as Paul defines it so clearly in 1 Corinthians 15:1-4 is self-evident; because in Matthew 10 the disciples knew NOTHING about His coming death! In fact when He informed them over a year later that *"He must be killed, and on the third day be raised to life,"* Peter took Him aside and began to rebuke Him. *"Never Lord!"* he said. *"This shall never happen to You!"* (Matthew 16:21-22). So when Peter was preaching the message of the Kingdom of God in Matthew 10 he certainly was not preaching the gospel of the grace of God! Anyway the message of Matthew 10 & Luke 9:2-3 was rescinded by the Lord Himself in Luke 22:36 when He said those most important words "BUT NOW…"

The key word in kingdom preaching is - repent. The key word in gospel preaching is - believe. The gospel of John does not once employ the word 'repentance' but John uses the verb 'believe' ninety-nine times! The Epistle to the Romans, does not use the word 'repentance' in connection with the saving of a soul, except in 2:4 where repentance is equivalent to salvation itself. *"When he comes, he will convict the world in regard to sin… because men do not believe in me"* (John 16:8-9).

The main thrust of the gospel of the Kingdom is to warn that the Kingdom to be set up by Jesus Christ, is NEAR.

This will be effectively accomplished by enlightened Jews during the tribulation period warning the world of the Lord's imminent return to set up his Kingdom.

As diagram 4 portrays in the left hand column, Matthew 24 refers to the Jewish remnant in Judea during the tribulation era, the features of the rapture in the right hand column are sharply distinguished from Matthew 24. As Sir Robert Anderson said, "Let us not forget that Matthew 24 & 25 relate to the coming of the SON OF MAN…. never once does the Lord's title of SON OF MAN occur in the epistles of the New Testament; never once is it used in Scripture in relation

MATHEW 24

TRIBULATION

- "THE SON OF MAN"
- SIGNS IN THE HEAVENS'
- JUDGMENTS
- INSTRUCTIONS FOR ESCAPE
- WARNINGS OF ANTICHRIST
- CHRIST COMES TO EARTH
- TRIBES OF THE EARTH MOURN
- PUBLIC - INVOLVES SINNERS
- NO RESURRECTION MENTIONED
- TWO CLASSES - JEWISH 'ELECT' AND SINFUL NATIONS
- TRUMPET BLOWN BY AN ANGEL
- ANGELS GATHER GOD'S ELECT
- BLESSING TO REMAIN FOR ENTRANCE INTO THE KINGDOM, THE REST BEING TAKEN AWAY IN JUDGMENT
- TIME INVOLVED
- PERIOD OF UNPARALLED ANGUISH

DIA. 4

RAPTURE

I THESSALONIANS 4

- "THE LORD HIMSELF"
- NO SIGNS OR WONDERS
- NO JUDGMENT
- NO PROVISION FOR ESCAPE
- ANTICHRIST NOT IN VIEW
- MEET HIM IN THE AIR"
- NO MOURNING
- PRIVATE - INVOLVES CHURCH
- "DEAD IN CHRIST SHALL RISE"
- TWO CLASSES - "THEM WHICH ARE ASLEEP" "WE WHICH ARE ALIVE"
- "TRUMP OF GOD"
- CHRIST HIMSELF
- BLESSING TO BE TAKEN IN RAPTURE, THOSE "OUT OF CHRIST" BEING LEFT TO GO THROUGH THE TRIBULATION.
- INSTANTANEOUS
- A MOMENT OF MARVELLOUS JOY

to the Church of God or the people of God of this dispensation. Surely this fact alone might save us from the error of confounding the Coming of the Son of Man for the deliverance of His earthly people and the judgement of living nations upon earth, with the coming of the Lord to call His heavenly people home, and to bring this "Christian Dispensation" to an end." (Forgotten Truths p.78).

CHAPTER ONE

Air Navigation - World War II

During the War I served as a navigator in Bomber Command on 214 Squadron, East Anglia. The Stirling aircraft we were flying proved one of the most important landmarks in the history of the R.A.F., for it was the first bomber to be received by that service capable of giving tangible expression of the Air Staff's beliefs in strategic bombing, and delivering in Winston Churchill's words, "the shattering strokes of retributive justice" and which played such a primary role in the defeat of the Axis powers.

Night flying over German-occupied-Europe in those days was more than observing a magnificent pyrotechnic spectacle. Navigation was arduous work mentally and physically - one had to plot on a mercator chart, each course and distance the aircraft flew. Ones position was found by several sextant shots on the stars, a tedious, laborious task. One's efforts were hampered by the heavy clothing worn, including silk and leather gloves, to protect from the cold at 15,000 feet; the oxygen mask that invariably dropped condensation on your chart - of course right where one was plotting! To add to the interest of your night out on the town, the desk delighted in the maddening habit of suddenly dropping half an inch then rising sharply, breaking yet another pencil point! All this little picnic was taking place in a cramped, confined, cold, dark, blacked-out space, with just a pencil light on an adjustable arm above one's desk, and the incessant roar from the four 1300 H.P. Bristol Hercules engines effectively drowning out any conversation except through your inter-com. There were no pressurised cabins in 1943!

In addition to these problems, there were the minor distractions of having to plot the evasive action taken to avoid the overly intimate attention those night fighters were paying us, to say nothing of the FLAK the gunners on the ground with their lethal 88mm anti-aircraft guns, and probing searchlights were throwing up at us - then of course, there was a real likelihood of a 4000 lb block-buster dropping through our ceiling from a friendly Halifax or Lancaster that could fly higher over the target area than our goodselves. Perhaps that is why they were called SHORT STIRLINGS - short in altitude! It was all called DEAD RECKONING - if you were not back on your squadron by 0500 hours you were RECKONED DEAD!!

Air Navigation Today (A.I.N.S. Area Inertial Navigation System)

How different is navigation today on say a modern D.C.10 aircraft.

The latitude and longitude co-ordinates of departure and destination are fed into the micro-electronic navigation computer on the aircraft. Then the latitude and longitude are established about every 300 miles along the route. They are called WAY POINTS. Every movement of the aircraft is measured and recorded by electric sensors, mounted on delicate gyroscopes. There are three of these inertial sensor platforms. Each measures the progress of the aircraft independently, and the aircraft computer keeps averaging the three results and presenting a continuous printout of the average of the three systems which it calculates five times per second. This is only one example of the new wonders of the microprocessor age.

The Bible's Navigation System (B.N.S.)

The B.N.S. Bible Navigation System also has three independent navigation systems to determine our destination. It also has WAY POINTS giving exact guidance to within a year over the last 2,590 years of history. It also has several minor back-up systems that unanimously and consistently print out, like the three major systems, the terminal YEAR 2005 AD.

Its amazing patterns and precise predictions makes an interlocking, harmonious and perfect picture, only when the canvas is completely painted up to the year 2005.

How excited are passengers as they draw near to their long expected destination. They put the magazines back in the rack, pack their handbags, freshen up, and try to tidy travel worn clothes. Well our E.T.A. (estimated time of arrival) is nearly up. Fasten your seatbelts, and prepare for the most exciting touch down in history!

The Briefing Room

Our squadron was tucked away in the remote village of Chedburgh, seven miles south of Bury St. Edmunds, Suffolk. In the afternoon we would go into the briefing room and prepare our maps and charts for the night's attack against the Nazi war machine. There boldly printed along the front wall were the words -

"KEEP ON TRACK - KEEP ON TIME -
KEEP ON LIVING"

So let me take you into the briefing room now and let us plot the three major bearings that converge into 2005 AD. Later we will look at the back up systems and the WAY points that confirm and converge into that year.

The Three Major Bearings (Dia.5)

1. The first bearing we will call the 'TIMES of the MILLENNIA'. This one is not directly stated in the Bible, but constantly hinted at and inferred from Genesis to Revelation. So at this stage we will say - the TIMES OF THE MILLENNIA is a STRONGLY, SUSPECTED POSSIBILITY.

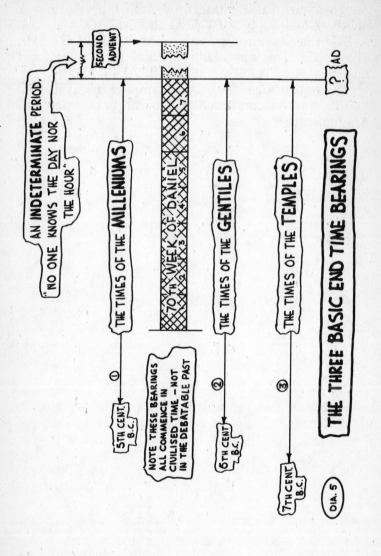

"AN INDETERMINATE PERIOD. NO ONE KNOWS THE DAY NOR THE HOUR"

SECOND ADVENT

THE TIMES OF THE MILLENIUMS

70TH WEEK OF DANIEL 1 2 3 4 5 6 7

THE TIMES OF THE GENTILES

THE TIMES OF THE TEMPLES

① 5TH CENT. B.C.

NOTE THESE BEARINGS ALL COMMENCE IN CIVILISED TIME — NOT IN THE DEBATABLE PAST

② 6TH CENT. B.C.

③ 7TH CENT. B.C.

? AD

THE THREE BASIC END TIME BEARINGS

DIA. 5

25

2. The next one we will call the 'TIMES of the GENTILES'. This period is categorically stated in black and white in the Biblical Navigation System, so we will call this one - THE TIMES OF THE GENTILES - A SURE, SPECIFIC, SCRIPTURAL PREDICTION.

3. The third bearing we will call the 'TIMES OF THE TEMPLES'. This one is deeply rooted in history, and reveals A STARTLING SYMMETRICAL PATTERN.

Note that all these bearings commence in CIVILISED TIMES, and are confirmed by Biblical, Babylonian and Assyrian records.

CHAPTER TWO

Bearing No 1,
"The Times of the Millennia"

In the first chapter of the Bible we learn that God brought order out of chaos in six days, and then rested on the seventh. The belief has persisted throughout the centuries that likewise on a scale of a day as a thousand years God would work for 6,000 years to restore blessing, and then rest for another 1000 years. *"Do not let this one fact escape you, that with the Lord one day is as a thousand years, and a thousand years as one day"* (2 Peter 3:8 Amp Bible).

Here are a couple of examples out of many.

Epistle of Barnabas 150 AD

"Even in the beginning of creation he makes mention of the Sabbath, and God made in six days the work of HIS hands, and HE finished them on the sixth day, and HE rested the seventh day and sanctified it. Consider, my children what that signifies... in six thousand years the Lord will bring all things to an end. For with Him one day is as a thousand years, as HIMSELF testifieth, saying 'Behold this day shall be a thousand years'. Therefore children, in six days, that is six thousand years, shall all things be accomplished."

Barnabas 12:1-5

Hippolytus 220 AD

"The six thousand years must needs be fulfilled that the Sabbath may come - even the rest, that Holy day on which God rested from all HIS works. The Sabbath then is a type and image of the future Kingdom of the Saints when they shall reign with Christ, after HIS coming down from Heaven, as John declares in the Apocalypse. *"For a day with the Lord is as a thousand years."*

Science recently substantiated this equation of a day equalling a thousand years. James Reid, a Scientist, in his book "God, the Atom, and the Universe" states:- "Time slows down as speed increases. If spacemen were travelling at or near the speed of light, and beamed their T.V. cameras on planet earth, over four days of our actions would be squeezed into one second of their time - they would only have to watch one of their days to see a thousand years of earth's history pass across their tube."

Maybe it's about time to do this with the Bible statements, for this is exactly the ratio of time difference that Peter tells us about in 2 Peter 3:8."
REMEMBER "GOD IS LIGHT."

Bible Chronology

Western minds regard chronology as a continuity of time, successive years linked together whether viewed backwards or forwards. But the Hebrews viewed and used chronology differently (See Appendix 1).

In Bible chronology there are definite GAPS - some apparent, others hidden; but most importantly all the years that God wants us to RECKON are REVEALED i.e. recorded. In Chronophecy we calculate, count the years forward into the future - as we will learn later when looking at the incredibly long years of Adam, Enoch and Methuselah. They all make sense if we view them as prophetic co-ordinates into the future, not historic signposts into the past. When one stops arguing over the ACTUAL and starts RECKONING on the REVEALED the light dawns bright and clear.

So counting the years that have not been hidden from us, the following pattern emerges. Confining ourselves to the duration of years REVEALED, rather than the real succession of years passed we have:-

28

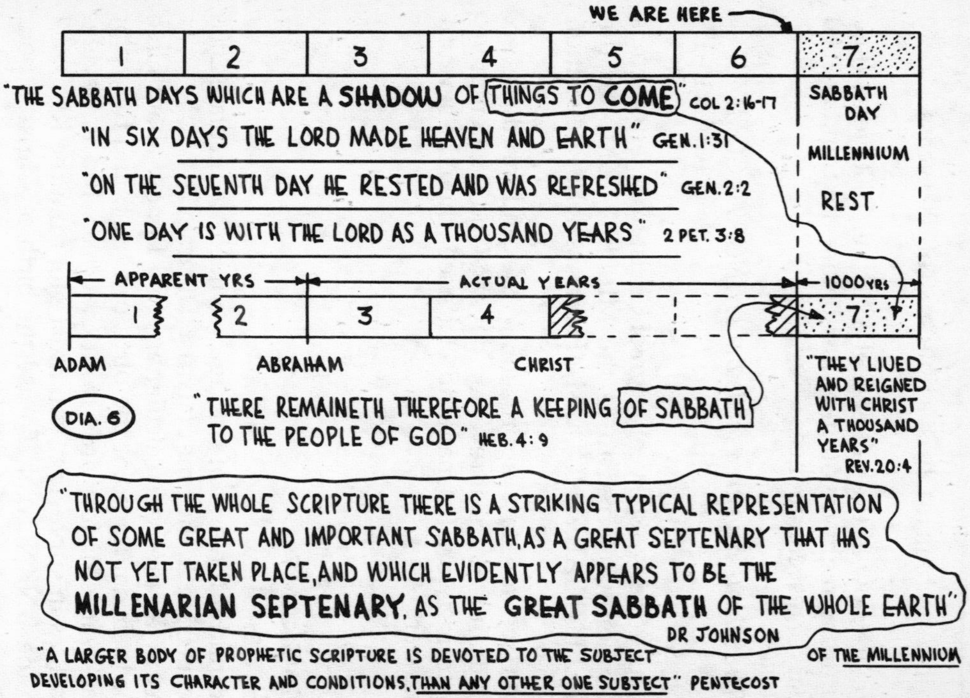

WE ARE HERE →

1	2	3	4	5	6	7

"THE SABBATH DAYS WHICH ARE A SHADOW OF (THINGS TO COME)" COL.2:16-17

"IN SIX DAYS THE LORD MADE HEAVEN AND EARTH" GEN.1:31

"ON THE SEVENTH DAY HE RESTED AND WAS REFRESHED" GEN.2:2

"ONE DAY IS WITH THE LORD AS A THOUSAND YEARS" 2 PET. 3:8

7 — SABBATH DAY / MILLENNIUM / REST

APPARENT YRS ← → ACTUAL YEARS

1	2	3	4

ADAM   ABRAHAM   CHRIST

DIA. 6

"THERE REMAINETH THEREFORE A KEEPING OF SABBATH TO THE PEOPLE OF GOD" HEB.4:9

1000 YRS — 7 — "THEY LIVED AND REIGNED WITH CHRIST A THOUSAND YEARS" REV.20:4

"THROUGH THE WHOLE SCRIPTURE THERE IS A STRIKING TYPICAL REPRESENTATION OF SOME GREAT AND IMPORTANT SABBATH, AS A GREAT SEPTENARY THAT HAS NOT YET TAKEN PLACE, AND WHICH EVIDENTLY APPEARS TO BE THE MILLENARIAN SEPTENARY, AS THE GREAT SABBATH OF THE WHOLE EARTH"
DR JOHNSON

"A LARGER BODY OF PROPHETIC SCRIPTURE IS DEVOTED TO THE SUBJECT OF THE MILLENNIUM DEVELOPING ITS CHARACTER AND CONDITIONS, THAN ANY OTHER ONE SUBJECT" PENTECOST

DIAGRAM 6 MILLENNIAL DAYS

From Adam to Abraham a time span of 2000 years.

From Abraham to Christ a time span of 2000 years.

We are now at the tail end of a further 2000 years (late Saturday night if you like) just before the Sunday 1000 years of rest commences. (Rev 20:5-6).

"The Sabbath days are a shadow of THINGS TO COME"
(Col 2:16-17)

This coming 1000 year reign of Christ from Jerusalem is commonly referred to as the MILLENNIUM - or the MILLENNIAL KINGDOM. (Hebrews 4:4,8; Revelation 20:5-6).

As we are fast approaching the end of these six thousands years of revealed days in God's redemptive, restoring work for mankind - let's see when the seventh will start.

DIAGRAM 7

To find B the end of this age we need to calculate 2000 years from A, the time of Christ (Diagram 7).

Now all previous calculations that I know about have for their datum point the birth of Christ, and they plot backwards or forwards from that year. But in navigation, as in surveying, you must plot from the KNOWN to the UNKNOWN. To use the birth of Christ is poor navigation for two reasons:-

a) Scholars are still divided over the precise date of HIS birth, their estimates vary by nineteen years.
b) The Bible emphasises the centrality of the CROSS - the DEATH of Christ, not HIS BIRTH!

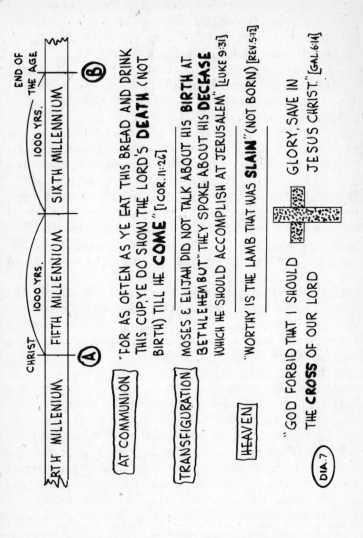

| 4TH MILLENIUM | FIFTH MILLENNIUM | SIXTH MILLENNIUM |
| | CHRIST 1000 YRS. | 1000 YRS. |

(A) ... (B)

END OF THE AGE

AT COMMUNION

"FOR AS OFTEN AS YE EAT THIS BREAD AND DRINK THIS CUP, YE DO SHOW THE LORD'S **DEATH** (NOT BIRTH) TILL HE **COME**" [I COR. 11:26]

TRANSFIGURATION

MOSES & ELIJAH DID NOT TALK ABOUT HIS **BIRTH** AT BETHLEHEM BUT "THEY SPOKE ABOUT HIS **DECEASE** WHICH HE SHOULD ACCOMPLISH AT JERUSALEM" [LUKE 9:31]

HEAVEN

"WORTHY IS THE LAMB THAT WAS **SLAIN**" (NOT BORN) [REV. 5:12]

"GOD FORBID THAT I SHOULD GLORY, SAVE IN THE **CROSS** OF OUR LORD JESUS CHRIST." [GAL. 6:14]

DIA. 7

31

For instance:-

a) At Communion *"For as often as ye eat this bread, and drink this cup, ye do show the Lord's DEATH (not birth) till HE come"* (1 Cor 11:26).

b) In Heaven they say *"Worthy is the Lamb that was SLAIN"* (not BORN) Revelation 5:12.

c) On the Mount of Transfiguration, Moses and Elijah did not talk about HIS BIRTH at BETHLEHEM but *"they spoke about HIS DECEASE which HE should accomplish at Jerusalem."* (Luke 9:31).

It is HIS DEATH not HIS BIRTH that determines our basic DATUM LINE. In the providence of God in 1977 a Cambridge scholar published the fruits of his research on "Chronological Aspects of the Life of Christ" H.W. Hoehner (Zondervan). He conclusively proves from history, astronomy and the famous prophecy in Daniel 9 that Christ died on FRIDAY 3RD APRIL 33 AD. (Dia. 8, see Appendix Two). This then is our definite datum point for plotting our bearings - add 2000 years to A and we have B. (Dia. 6).

But these 2000 years are not our solar years of 365.2421 days! The Hebrews measured duration by the moon not the sun. They used a 360 day year as was used in Daniel's prophecy to find when "Messiah would be cut off" (Daniel 9:26) See Appendix II.

As the great Sir Isaac Newton pointed out:-

"All nations, before the just length of the solar year was known, reckoned months by the course of the moon, and the years by the return of winter, summer, spring and autumn, and in making calendars for their festivals, they reckoned thirty days to a lunar month, and twelve lunar months to a year, taking the nearest round numbers, whence came the division of the ecliptic into 360 degrees". (The Coming Prince Sir Robert Anderson p.68).

$12 \times 30 = 360$ days, the prophetic year.

To convert 1000 prophetic years of 360 days each, into solar years all we do is this:- $1000 \times 360 \div 365.24 = 986$ years to the nearest round number.

32

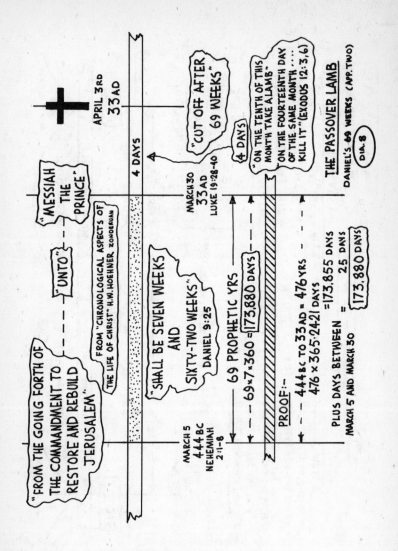

"FROM THE GOING FORTH OF THE COMMANDMENT TO RESTORE AND REBUILD JERUSALEM"

"UNTO"

"MESSIAH THE PRINCE"

FROM "CHRONOLOGICAL ASPECTS OF THE LIFE OF CHRIST" H.W. HOEHNER ZONDERVAN

"SHALL BE SEVEN WEEKS AND SIXTY-TWO WEEKS" DANIEL 9:25

69 PROPHETIC YRS

69 × 7 × 360 = 173,880 DAYS

"CUT OFF AFTER 69 WEEKS"

4 DAYS

APRIL 3RD 33 AD

MARCH 30 33AD LUKE 19:28-40

MARCH 5 444BC NEHEMIAH 2:11-8

4 DAYS

"ON THE TENTH OF THIS MONTH TAKE A LAMB" "ON THE FOURTEENTH DAY OF THE SAME MONTH .... KILL IT" (EXODUS 12:3,6)

THE PASSOVER LAMB

DANIEL'S 69 WEEKS (APP. TWO)

DIA. 8

PROOF:-

444BC TO 33AD = 476YRS
476 × 365·2421 DAYS = 173,855 DAYS

PLUS DAYS BETWEEN MARCH 5 AND MARCH 30 = 25 DAYS

173,880 DAYS

33

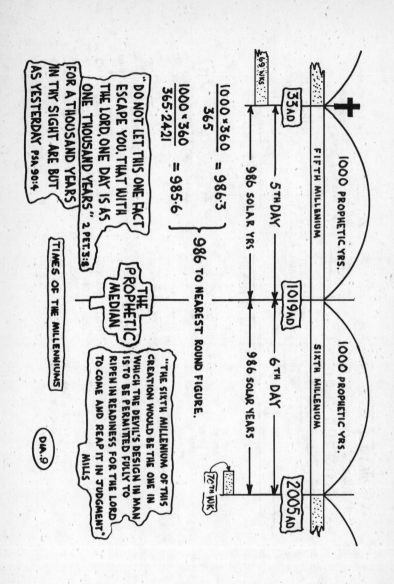

1000 PROPHETIC YRS.

FIFTH MILLENIUM

1000 PROPHETIC YRS.

SIXTH MILLENIUM

33 AD

69 WKS

1019 AD

THE PROPHETIC MEDIAN

2005 AD

70TH WK

5TH DAY

986 SOLAR YRS

6TH DAY

986 SOLAR YEARS

$$\frac{1000 \times 360}{365} = 986.3$$

$$\left.\begin{array}{l}\dfrac{1000 \times 360}{365} = 986.3 \\[2mm] \dfrac{1000 \times 360}{365 \cdot 2421} = 985.6\end{array}\right\} \; 986 \text{ TO NEAREST ROUND FIGURE.}$$

"DO NOT LET THIS ONE FACT ESCAPE YOU, THAT WITH THE LORD, ONE DAY IS AS ONE THOUSAND YEARS, AND A THOUSAND YEARS IN THY SIGHT ARE BUT AS YESTERDAY" PSA. 90:4

"THE SIXTH MILLENIUM OF THIS CREATION WOULD BE THE ONE IN WHICH THE DEVIL'S DESIGN IN MAN IS TO BE PERMITTED FULLY TO RIPEN IN READINESS FOR THE LORD TO COME AND REAP IT IN JUDGMENT" MILLS

TIMES OF THE MILLENNIUMS

DIA. 9

DIAGRAM 9 TIMES OF THE MILLENNIA

So we come, by adding two prophetic millennia on to 33 AD, to our terminus - 2005 AD! This bearing we call the TIMES OF THE MILLENNIA - a strongly suspected possibility is all we can say at this stage. (DIA.9)

Now no navigator can plot his course on one bearing, as would-be prophetic pundits did last century (p. 12-14)Non-fulfilment of their predictions brought the marvellous chronophecy (chronological prophecy) of the Bible into disrepute. We need at least two, preferably three bearings, to know definitely where we are on the vast sea of time. As Jesus said - *"In the mouth of TWO or THREE witnesses shall every word be established"* (Matthew 18:16).

We will find there are more than the three major bearings pointing to the year 2005 AD. There are also the Times of the Patriarchs and the Times of the Anti-Diluvians. Believe it or not, Abraham, Noah and Moses all direct us to 2005, not forgetting Adam!

FOR BIBLE STUDENTS

Here are some scriptures that fit comfortably into this Millennial pattern:
Hosea 6:1-2; Joshua 3:4 (K.J.V.); Matthew 17:1-2; Luke 10:35 with Matthew 20:2; Luke 13:32; John 2:1; 4:43; 11:6-7
There are many more types of this septenary plan!

CHAPTER THREE
Bearing No 2,
The Times of the Gentiles

I am indebted to the book "The End of the Days" by A.E. Bloomfield (p. 50-54) published 1961, for some of the material in this section. He came up with the year 2004. If he had correctly calculated from BC years to AD years, he would have come to 2005 AD.

Our second bearing derives its name from the words of Christ in Luke 21:24 *"Jerusalem will be trampled on by the Gentiles until the times of the Gentiles are fulfilled."* It refers to a period of time when Jerusalem is or could be subject to Gentile power.

Jewish Jerusalem first became subject to Gentile power during the period when the Babylonian Empire was supreme (624 BC - 539 BC). In a series of progressive judgments (servitude, captivity and finally desolation), Nebuchadnezzar, King of Babylon, besieged Jerusalem on three occasions (605, 597 and 586 BC). Many Jews were taken into captivity including Daniel (606 BC) and later on, Ezekiel (597 BC). Daniel reveals the CHARACTER of the TIMES OF THE GENTILES, (chaps. 2 and 7). Ezekiel reveals their CHRONOLOGY.

The key to the "TIMES OF THE GENTILES" dominating and treading down Jerusalem is found in Ezekiel's prophecies. The pivot around which his book centres is the destruction of Jerusalem (chaps. 1-24) which occurred in 586 BC. In Ezekiel chapter four, we find the key to how long the Gentiles would have actual or potential control over Jerusalem; put another way, how long the children of Israel would be driven and dispersed amongst the Gentiles.

"In this way, the people of Israel will eat defiled bread among the GENTILES where I will drive them."(v:13).

Just as an opera star tells a story by singing, and a ballet star by dancing, so Ezekiel had to act out the coming fall of Jerusalem. In drama fashion God had him act the fate of the city and of the time the children of Israel would be dispersed amongst the Gentiles.

In the first four verses he is instructed to draw the city of Jerusalem on a clay tablet, then make a model of it under siege, complete with battering rams, a ramp and the camp of the besieging soldiers surrounding it. God then commanded Ezekiel *"lie on your left side and put the sin of the house of Israel upon yourself. You are to bear their sin for the number of days you lie on your side. I have assigned you the same number of days as the years of their sin. So for 390 days, you will bear the sin of the house of Israel.*

"After you have finished this, lie down again, this time on your right side, and bear the sin of the house of Judah. I have assigned you 40 days, a day for each year."(v.4-6).

So here is the prophetic picture:- (DIA 10)

  390 days - iniquity of Israel
+   40 days - iniquity of Judah
_____

= 430 days - full period of punishment

"I have appointed each day for a year"

Therefore 430 years is the full period of punishment, commencing from the siege of Jerusalem 586 BC. From this 430 years we must subtract the 70 years of punishment in Babylon (Jeremiah 29:10, 25:11; 2 Chronicles 36:21), giving a period of 360 years of further punishment after the 70 years had run their course. After 70 years there was repentance amongst some Jews. The balance of 360 years involves the Jews who remained in exile.

But after these 360 years i.e. 156 BC the exiled Jews were still unrepentant. (DIA 10)

2005AD

B.C.516   B.C.584

70 YRS   FINAL RETURN

360 × 7 = 2520 YRS

"JERUSALEM WILL BE TRAMPLED ON BY THE GENTILES UNTIL THE TIMES OF THE GENTILES BE FULFILLED" (LUKE 21:24)

DESTRUCTION JERUSALEM FINAL CAPTIVITY

"390 DAYS SHALT THOU BEAR THE INIQUITY OF THE HOUSE OF ISRAEL

40 " " " " " - JUDAH" (EZEK.4:1-8)

430 " FULL PERIOD OF PUNISHMENT.

"I HAVE APPOINTED EACH DAY FOR A YEAR. EVEN THUS SHALL THE CHILDREN OF ISRAEL EAT THEIR DEFILED BREAD AMONG THE GENTILES WHITHER I WILL DRIVE THEM" (EZEK 4)

430 YRS FULL PERIOD OF PUNISHMENT.

— 70 YRS ALREADY PUNISHED IN BABYLON "AFTER 70 YRS BE ACCOMPLISHED AT BABYLON I WILL VISIT YOU... CAUSING YOU TO RETURN TO THIS PLACE" (JER.29:10)

360 YRS

"IF YE WILL NOT FOR ALL THIS HEARKEN UNTO ME, THEN I WILL PUNISH YOU SEVEN TIMES MORE FOR YOUR SINS" (LEV.26:18)

360 × 7 = 2520 YRS.

THE TIMES OF THE GENTILES

DIA.10

So there is an additional factor to be added to this prophecy if it is to make any sense. God deliberately hid these missing years as he did not want the knowledge revealed until the end time. In the next book after Ezekiel we read, *"the words are closed up and sealed until the time of the end"*(Daniel 12:9). In the book preceding Ezekiel, in the context of Israel's final return to the land we read, *"In days to come you will understand this"*(Jeremiah 30:24). In the end times we must expect increased illumination, not further revelation (Revelation 22:18-19). *"But you, O Daniel, shut up the words and seal the book until the time of the end. Then many shall run to and fro, and search anxiously through the Book, and knowledge of God's purposes as revealed by HIS prophets shall be increased and come great.* (Daniel 12:4 Amplified Bible)

"It is the glory of God to conceal a thing, but the glory of Kings is to search a thing out." (Proverbs 25:2)

The missing factor is found in Leviticus 26 where we find the identical context to Ezekiel's prophecy e.g. siege conditions (v.26 - 29) dispersal amongst the Gentiles (v.33) - *"I will scatter you among the nations"*, plus desolation of their cities, and the land laid waste. Four times in the section on their punishment for disobedience (v.14–39) we find our missing factor - *"If after this you will not listen to me, I will punish you for your sins SEVEN TIMES OVER"* (v.18,21,24 and 28).

We found out earlier, that projecting 360 years from 516 BC, only landed us in a void, a prophetic no man's land. But if we bring in the hidden factor it all becomes crystal clear. *"I will multiply your afflictions SEVEN times over"* (Leviticus 26:21) 360 x 7 = 2520 years.

Adding 2520 years to 516 BC brings us again, as in the times of the MILLENNIA to the year 2005 AD! (DIA.10)

For those of you who have problems correctly calculating across BC/AD refer to Appendix 3.

19th Century Writers

Last century, writers on prophecy inevitably used the

2520 years from the fall of Jerusalem in 586 BC and came to 1935 A.D. as the terminal year for the Times of the Gentiles. Their failure to see that the Times of the Gentiles is not 2520 years but 2590 (2520 + 70) years is the basic cause why older generation Christians today, who saw the non-fulfilment of their hopes in the early '30's, and who today should be on their tip toes (even if they are now arthritic!) of anticipation, are now sceptical, and even antagonistic, to chronophecy, the most marvellous and accurate guiding light God has given us for this final home stretch of man's government of our planet earth.

We have just demonstrated that adding 2590 solar years of (365.24 days to a year) leads us to 2005 A.D. (DIA.12). Now an amazing fact emerges if we convert these 2590 years into prophetic years, and measure from 586 BC. A prophetic year as we saw in the Times of the Millennia is one of 360 days in duration. So we have $2590 \times 360 \div 365.24 = 2552$ solar years.
Therefore:-
586 BC + 2590 prophetic years
= 586 BC + 2552 solar years
= 1967 AD! (DIA.11)
The very year Israel recaptured old Jerusalem and the temple area, in the Six Day War from the Arabs! So bearing number two has a double significance pointing to 1967 and 2005 AD! We will learn later (p.169) that bearing number one also has a double significance.

Some contemporary prophetic writers believe that 1967 was the end of the Times of the Gentiles, because of present Jewish independence and control of the city of Jerusalem and the temple area. But the multi-metallic image in Daniel 2 picturing Gentile sovereignty is not destroyed until the falling stone (Christ) smashes into the toes and the Lord sets up HIS everlasting Kingdom (Daniel 2:44-45). Jerusalem is yet to be trodden down of

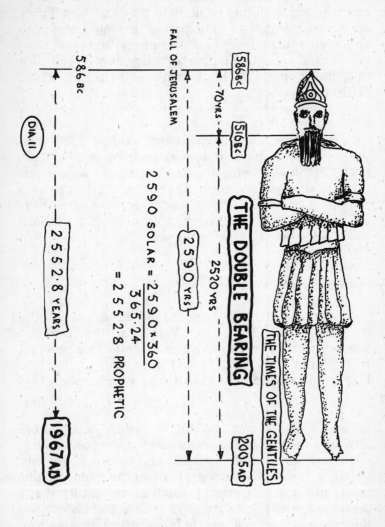

FALL OF JERUSALEM

586 BC

586 BC

- 70 YRS -

516 BC

2590 YRS

2520 YRS

THE DOUBLE BEARING

THE TIMES OF THE GENTILES

2005 AD

DIA. 11

2552.8 YEARS

1967 AD

$$\frac{2590 \text{ SOLAR} = 2590 \times 360}{365.24} = 2552.8 \text{ PROPHETIC}$$

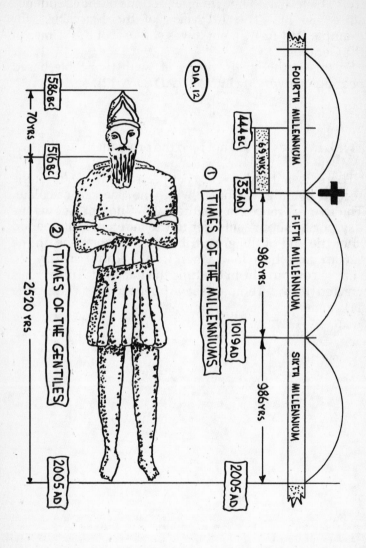

DIA. 12

① TIMES OF THE MILLENNIUMS

② TIMES OF THE GENTILES

FOURTH MILLENNIUM

FIFTH MILLENNIUM

SIXTH MILLENNIUM

444 BC

69 WKS

33 AD

986 YRS

1019 AD

986 YRS

2005 AD

586 BC

70 YRS

516 BC

2520 YRS

2005 AD

43

the Gentiles for 3.5 years (Revelation 11:2) and then, the end (2005 AD) comes. See also Zechariah 14:2. The Dome of the Rock is still under Moslem (GENTILE) control! The Jews had known brief periods of independence since 586 BC. The 101 years of the Maccabees for example (164-63 BC), but it was still part of the 'Times of the Gentiles.'

So this is the stage we are at, with two Bible based bearings converging into 2005 AD (DIA.12).

N.B. In case you did not read the prologue!

There is a hidden gap between 2005 AD and the second coming of Christ, which no one can calculate. The five references in Matthew 24 - ''no one knows the day nor the hour'' all refer to the indeterminate period after the end of the great tribulation. If He came on the 1260th day, those living then would 'know the day' by simple counting from the time the image of Antichrist is erected in the Temple (see Appendix four, also page 11).

CHAPTER FOUR

Bearing No 3,
The Times of the Temples

We have seen two Bible bearings converge into 2005 AD and will see several more later. We are now going to see a very thrilling one, deeply rooted in history, perfectly symmetrical, converging into 2005 AD. When the Lord revealed this bearing to me in December 1985 - I felt more excited than Columbus sighting land, or Sir Edmund Hillary conquering Mt. Everest. I knew then, beyond all doubt, that 2005 AD was all I suspected it to be - the end of man's government of this planet. Subsequent discoveries have only confirmed this view.

Historic Dates

As we look at the symmetry of time in connection with Zion, Mt. Moriah, and the temple area, we will be dealing with dates. The eight dates are all within the time of written records - there is no debate about them amongst the scholars, whether conservative or liberal in outlook. They are all easily verified, and have not been manipulated in any way to fit a pattern or suit a theory.

Professor Edwin Thiele of Chicago University, in his magnificent book ''The Mysterious Numbers of the Hebrew Kings'', demonstrates the absolute accuracy of the chronologies of the Kings of Israel and Judah. On page 22 he writes:- ''The chronologist must keep in mind, that it is his task, not to manufacture history, but to recover history. In dealing with chronology, he is dealing with something fundamental and absolute; something altogether fixed, that allows no deviation in any way, even by a single year, if it is to be entirely correct. Adjustments cannot be made, a little here and a little there, in order to secure some desired result.

Events happened as they did, and when they did, and the task of the chronologist is to fit those events into their exact niches in history. Carefully and correctly performed, the chronologist's work will, when finished, comprise a complete and harmonious pattern, consistent with itself and in perfect harmony with the correct chronological pattern of all nations round about.''

Getting Started

What triggered off this line of thought was reading in "The Witness of the Stars", published in 1893, that if one plots back 1260 years from the time Jerusalem fell to Islam in 637 AD, one comes to 624 BC the founding year of the Babylonian Empire; and plotting forwards, one comes to 1897 AD. These same figures were published earlier in 1886 "Light for the Last Days," by Grattan Guinness. On p.283 the author says "the remaining solar termination is still eleven years distant, 1897 AD. What is it likely to witness? Some more final and fatal fall of Ottoman power? Or some more distinct stage of Jewish restoration? Or both? Time will declare.''

Well, time has declared with a loud voice - August 29th 1897 was the historic opening of the first Zionist Congress in Basle, Switzerland, under the dynamic leadership of Theodore Herzl.

Let's Plot Backwards (Dia.13)

Projecting forwards 1260 years from 637 AD proved to be correct. My interest was now aroused to check out the 624 date, by plotting 1260 years backwards. Was it chronologically accurate, or just manipulated to suit a theory? Checking out, I found historians varied the start of the Babylonian Empire from 626 to 624 BC Surprisingly all are correct. In Babylonian chronology, the year a King comes to the throne is called his accession year. In this case Nabopolassar, the first King of Babylon came to the throne about March of our year 626

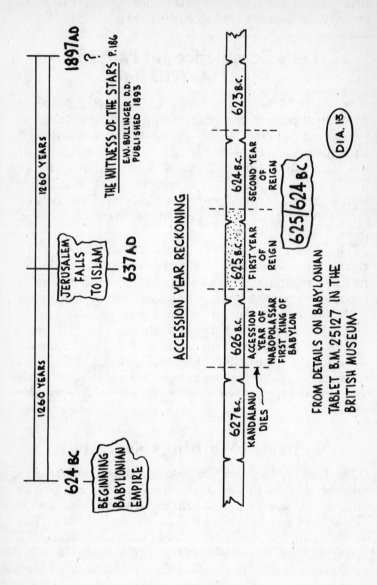

THE WITNESS OF THE STARS P.186
E.W. BULLINGER D.D.
PUBLISHED 1893

1897 AD ?

1260 YEARS

JERUSALEM FALLS TO ISLAM
637 AD

1260 YEARS

624 BC

BEGINNING BABYLONIAN EMPIRE

ACCESSION YEAR RECKONING

627 B.C.

KANDALANU DIES

626 B.C.
ACCESSION YEAR OF NABOPOLASSAR FIRST KING OF BABYLON

625 B.C.
FIRST YEAR OF REIGN

624 B.C.
SECOND YEAR OF REIGN

625/624 BC

623 B.C.

DIA. 13

FROM DETAILS ON BABYLONIAN TABLET B.M. 25127 IN THE BRITISH MUSEUM

47

BC. The next twelve months AFTER the accession year i.e. from March 625 to March 624 is recognised as the first year of his reign. This is confirmed by the arch-aeologist's find of the Babylonian tablet B.M. 25127.

Let's Commence our Pattern - Step One (Dia.14)

If we start plotting from early 624 BC we discover a wonderful pattern of equal proportional time spans in years emerge. Only an omnipotent God could design such historical symmetry. In 586 BC the commander of the Babylonian Imperial guard destroyed the city of Jerusalem and Solomon's temple, that had been standing for 380 years (Jeremiah 52:12-13). This gives us our first time span of 38 years in this symmetrical time plan of temple history.

The fall of Jerusalem and the loss of their temple, was a calamitous, catastrophic disaster of the first magnitude. Its fires are smoke signals, warning the world of what is shortly to come to pass, when God finally intervenes with radical surgery during the seven year lead-up to 2005 AD. More about that period later!

Jeremiah had warned his people for 40 years from 626 BC until the destruction of Jerusalem in 586 BC. Is it a coincidence that Jesus commenced his ministry in 30 AD and Herod's temple was destroyed exactly 40 years later in 70 AD?

Repeated Warnings Neglected

"The Lord God of their fathers, sent word through HIS messengers, AGAIN and AGAIN, because HE had pity on HIS people, and on HIS dwelling place. But they mocked God's messengers, despised HIS words, and scoffed at HIS prophets, until the wrath of the Lord was aroused against HIS people, and there was NO REMEDY" (2 Chronicles 36:15)

"Though I taught them AGAIN and AGAIN, they turned their backs to me and not their faces, they would not listen or

"ON THE TENTH DAY OF THE FIFTH MONTH, IN THE NINETEENTH YEAR OF NEBUCHADNEZZAR, KING OF BABYLON, NEBUZARADAN COMMANDER OF THE IMPERIAL GUARD, WHO SERVED THE KING OF BABYLON, CAME TO JERUSALEM. HE SET FIRE TO THE **TEMPLE OF THE LORD**, THE ROYAL PALACE, AND ALL THE HOUSES OF JERUSALEM. EVERY IMPORTANT BUILDING HE BURNED DOWN " [JER. 52:12-13]

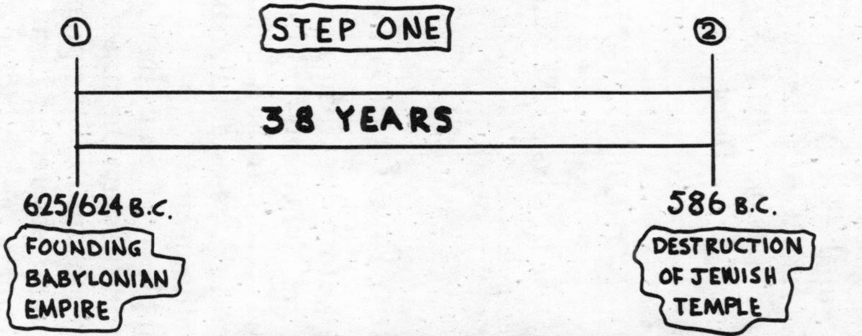

STEP ONE

38 YEARS

① 625/624 B.C.
FOUNDING BABYLONIAN EMPIRE

② 586 B.C.
DESTRUCTION OF JEWISH TEMPLE

THE TIMES OF THE TEMPLES ①

DIA. 14

49

respond to discipline.'' (Jeremiah 32:33)

"But I have spoken to you AGAIN and AGAIN, yet you have not obeyed me. AGAIN and AGAIN I sent all my servants the prophets to you.''(Jeremiah 35:14-15)

"For they have not listened to my words, declared the Lord, words that I sent to them AGAIN and AGAIN by my servants the prophets and you exiles have not listened either.'' (Jeremiah 29:19)

"AGAIN and AGAIN I sent my servants the prophets, who said do not this detestable thing that I hate. But they did not listen or pay attention; they did not turn from their wickedness.'' (Jeremiah 44:4-5)

"AGAIN and AGAIN they put God to the test.....in spite of all this they kept on sinning, in spite of HIS wonders, they did not believe. So HE ended their days in futility'' (Psalms 78:41,32)

NO RESPONSE - NO REMEDY

"A man who remains STIFF-NECKED after many rebukes will suddenly be destroyed - without remedy.'' (Proverbs 29:1)

Step Two In Our Pattern (Dia.15)

Three books form the closing sections of Old Testament history-Ezra, Nehemiah and Esther. They tell the story of the Jews' return from Babylon, the rebuilding of the temple, and the re-establishment of the Jews' national life in their homeland.

The temple was built first when Zerubbabel was governor and Joshua the priest. Later when Nehemiah was governor and Ezra the priest, the wall was rebuilt, and Jerusalem restored as a fortified city.

The account of the rebuilding of the temple is recorded in Ezra (chapters 3-6) where we read :- "They finished building the temple according to the command of the God of Israel and the decrees of Cyrus, Darius and Artaxerxes, Kings of Persia. The temple was completed on the third day of the month Adar, in the sixth year of King Darius'' (Ezra 6:14-15)

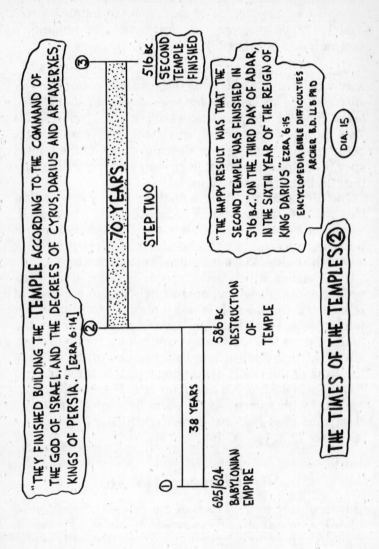

"THEY FINISHED BUILDING THE TEMPLE ACCORDING TO THE COMMAND OF THE GOD OF ISRAEL, AND THE DECREES OF CYRUS, DARIUS AND ARTAXERXES, KINGS OF PERSIA." [EZRA 6:14]

③ 516 BC
SECOND TEMPLE FINISHED

70 YEARS

STEP TWO

② 586 BC
DESTRUCTION OF TEMPLE

"THE HAPPY RESULT WAS THAT THE SECOND TEMPLE WAS FINISHED IN 516 B.C. ON THE THIRD DAY OF ADAR, IN THE SIXTH YEAR OF THE REIGN OF KING DARIUS." EZRA 6:15
ENCYCLOPEDIA BIBLE DIFFICULTIES
ARCHER B.D. LL.B PH.D

DIA. 15

38 YEARS

① 625/624
BABYLONIAN EMPIRE

THE TIMES OF THE TEMPLES ②

51

Darius came to the throne in 521 BC. So his sixth year, the year the temple was completed, was 516 BC. The following year 515 BC it was dedicated. Now we have the vital information for our second step, the date the Temple was completed-516 BC, giving us a time span of exactly 70 years from the destruction of Solomon's temple in 586 BC. (Dia 15)

Isaiah prophesied 150 years before the Persian King was ever born - *"Cyrus is my shepherd and shall perform all my pleasure; even saying to Jerusalem thou shalt be built; and to the TEMPLE, thy foundations shall be laid"* (Isaiah 44:28) This miracle of prediction was made 100 years at least before the first temple was destroyed. A Gentile king is specifically named, and it even states he will inaugurate the building of a second temple.

One of the strongest credentials of Jesus Christ is that He was pre-announced in incredible detail before HE was ever born. There is not a single prediction about Buddha, Socrates, Confucius, Laotze, Mohammed, or any of the modern Eastern gurus, before their births.

The Persian Kings were more humane than their predecessors, the Assyrian and Babylonian Kings, and repatriated the Jews. It is not without significance that while Assyria and Babylon have been erased from the maps, Persia still exists as a nation Iran, though tragically now, anti-Jewish. It is listed as one of the allies of the King of the north, when he attacks Israel in the last days (Ezekiel 38:5). No doubt modern Persia will go into oblivion with ancient Assyria and Babylon. *"I will bless them that bless thee and curse them that curse thee."* - (Genesis 12:3, Jer. 30:16)

Step Three (Dia. 16)

Our third step in the Times of the Temples, brings us to 70 AD, a time span of 585 years from 516 BC. Providing another part of the harmonious pattern that will eventually emerge.

70 AD saw not only Jerusalem and the Temple

destroyed as in 586 BC, but this marks the beginning of the word-wide dispersion of Jewry. Jesus weeping over Jerusalem said - *"The days will come when your enemies will build an embankment against you and encircle you, and hem you in on every side. They will dash you to the ground, you and the children within your walls. They will not leave one stone upon another, because you DID NOT RECOGNISE THE TIME OF GOD'S COMING TO YOU."* (Luke 19:41-44)

He also said, *"When you see Jerusalem surrounded by armies you will know that its desolation is near....there will be great distress in the land and wrath against this people. They will fall by the sword, and will be taken as prisoners to all the nations. Jerusalem will be trampled on until the times of the nations are fulfilled."* (Luke 21:20-24).

He said specifically concerning the temple *"See ye not all these buildings of the temple...there shall not be left here one stone upon another that shall not be thrown down."* (Matthew 24: 1-2).

For four years the beleaguered Jews desperately kept off the Roman armies of Titus. "The end was inevitable. With battering rams and portable bridges the Romans stormed the walls of Jerusalem. Like termites they spilled into the city, slaughtering a populace reduced to helplessness by starvation. Four years of bitter defeats at the hands of the Jews had made mockery of the vaunted invincibility of the Roman legions, and only killing could now soothe their bruised vanity. The temple was put to the torch, infants thrown into the flames, women raped, priests massacred, zealots thrown from the wall. Survivors of the carnage were earmarked for the triumphal procession to be held in Rome, sold for slaves, held for the wild beasts in the arenas, or saved to be thrown off the Tarpeian Rock in Rome for amusement. At no time did the Romans more justly earn the grim words of their own historian Laeitus who said "They make a desolation and call it peace." Altogether, Laeitus estimates 600,000 defenceless Jewish civilians were slain in the aftermath of the siege." (Jews, God and History. Max 1 Dimont p.106)

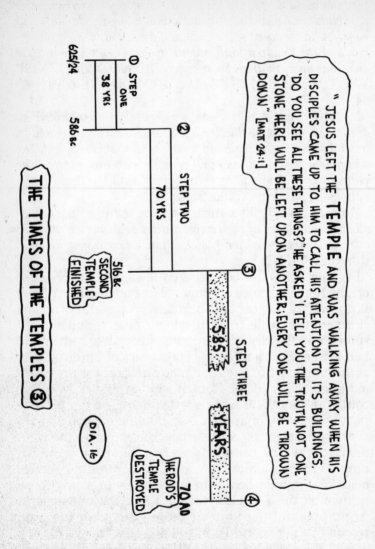

THE TIMES OF THE TEMPLES ③

"JESUS LEFT THE TEMPLE AND WAS WALKING AWAY WHEN HIS DISCIPLES CAME UP TO HIM TO CALL HIS ATTENTION TO ITS BUILDINGS. 'DO YOU SEE ALL THESE THINGS?' HE ASKED.'I TELL YOU THE TRUTH, NOT ONE STONE HERE WILL BE LEFT UPON ANOTHER; EVERY ONE WILL BE THROWN DOWN.'" [MATT. 24:1]

① STEP ONE — 625/24 — 38 YRS — 586 BC

② STEP TWO — 70 YRS — 516 BC SECOND TEMPLE FINISHED

③ STEP THREE — 585 YEARS

④ 70 AD HEROD'S TEMPLE DESTROYED

DIA. 1c

54

This appalling destruction and dispersion world-wide was due to their steadfast refusal to recognise and receive their Messiah, Jesus Christ the Son of Man. *"He came unto HIS own, and HIS own received HIM not."* (John 1:11)

This tragic page from history will shortly be re-enacted on a world-wide scale, when God's armies besiege and take planet earth. You either bow to Jesus Christ now and become conformed to HIS image (Romans 8:29) or are forced to bow to the Antichrist shortly and bear his image, which will bring physical disaster and ultimately eternal banishment from the presence of God and HIS people (Revelation 13:16-17; 20:10-15). This siege was predicted in Deuteronomy 28:49-68.

Step Four (Dia. 17)

Our fourth step brings us to the apex and central date in the marvellous multilateral pattern of the temples. You may be interested to know how I came upon this date. First I should make it clear that despite all my hard work, study, research and calculations I have been very conscious of the Holy Spirit - the Spirit of truth performing the ministry Christ said HE would - *"when HE is come....HE will show you THINGS TO COME."* (John 16:13) Without HIS guidance, shedding light on the Word of God, I would still be floundering in total darkness or misguided light. TO HIM BE ALL GLORY!

Last century prophetic writers knew that the Moslem conquest of Jerusalem in 637 AD (Gibbon's decline and fall of the Roman empire) was midpoint between the founding of Babylon in 624 BC and the future date of 1897 AD, which they anticipated would be of great significance.

This set me thinking. By now I was well aware from the first two bearings that the year 624 BC was the terminus a quo, and 2005 AD the terminus ad quem. The beginning and the end, the alpha and the omega.

I remembered Moslem power was pivotal to

THE TIMES OF THE TEMPLES ④

DIA.17

624 BC
586 BC

① 38 YRS

② 70 YRS

516 BC

③ 585 YEARS

70 AD

④ STEP FOUR

621 YRS.

ARABS

691 AD

⑤ DOME OF THE ROCK COMPLETED

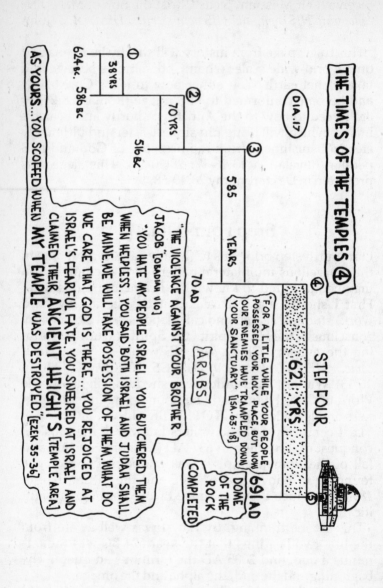

"FOR A LITTLE WHILE YOUR PEOPLE POSSESSED YOUR HOLY PLACE, BUT NOW OUR ENEMIES HAVE TRAMPLED DOWN YOUR SANCTUARY." [ISA. 63:18]

"THE VIOLENCE AGAINST YOUR BROTHER JACOB [OBADIAH v 10] ...
"YOU HATE MY PEOPLE ISRAEL... YOU BUTCHERED THEM WHEN HELPLESS... YOU SAID 'BOTH ISRAEL AND JUDAH SHALL BE MINE. WE WILL TAKE POSSESSION OF THEM. WHAT DO WE CARE THAT GOD IS THERE... YOU REJOICED AT ISRAEL'S FEARFUL FATE. YOU SNEERED AT ISRAEL AND CLAIMED THEIR ANCIENT HEIGHTS [TEMPLE AREA] AS YOURS... YOU SCOFFED WHEN MY TEMPLE WAS DESTROYED." [EZEK 35-36]

56

nineteenth century prophetic thinking, so decided to establish the central year between 624 BC and 2005 AD. I then investigated whether any important event connected with the Moslems or the temple area occurred in that year.

My calculator soon flashed up the central, bisecting year - 691 AD. Did it have any significance? I was hesitant and fearful, but finally opened my history books and there it was in black and white. "The Moslem Dome of the Rock was completed in 691 AD." I rechecked my calculations - it seemed too good to be true, but the calculator reflashed 691, 691, 691 AD! Maybe my history books were wrong. I dashed to the reference section of our local library. All the books echoed in one unanimous chorus 691, 691, 691 AD!!

I was beside myself with joy, the tears freely flowing. Our sovereign Lord had structured events into a perfect symmetrical pattern. Even though He had shown me only the first half, I was sure the rest of the pattern would unfold in a similar fashion. I could only cry out in the words of Isaiah *"O Lord, you are my God; I will exalt you and praise your name, for in perfect faithfulness, you have done marvellous things, things planned long ago."* (Isaiah 25:1).

The Dome of the Rock

This building is still mistakenly called by many, "The Mosque of Omar". After conquering Jerusalem, 637/638 AD, the Caliph Omar erected a temporary structure on the sight. This was replaced by Caliph Abdel Malik - he engaged architects from the Eastern Roman Empire. Thus on the very temple site there now stands in stone a monument of the merging of the Roman and Mohammedan Empires. Between 1938 and 1943, its columns were replaced with marble from Italy - (prophetic students of Daniel's image take note!)

This site and building is the most sensitive piece of real estate in the world; any wrong move here, could trigger off a world war. The rocky outcrop, over which the

Dome of the Rock has been built, was the site of the main altar in the Jewish Temple courtyard, and by 691 AD was already richly endowed with 17 centuries of Jewish tradition.

The Crusades

In the tenth century the Crusaders captured Jerusalem and the Dome of the Rock became the Templum Domini (Temple of our Lord) and the Crescent summounting the Dome was replaced with a Cross. It was recaptured by the Arabs in the next century. It could possibly be the Temple of Antichrist during his three and a half year reign of terror preceding 2005 AD.

God's feelings about the Dome of the Rock

"The violence against your brother Jacob" Obadiah v 10.
"You hate my people Israel… you butchered them when help-less… you said both Israel and Judah shall be mine. We will take possession of them. What do we care that God is there… you rejoiced at Israel's fearful fate (70 AD) *you sneered at Israel and claimed their ancient heights* (Mt Moriah 2,425 feet above sea level) *as yours….you scoffed when MY TEMPLE was destroyed!!* (Ezekiel 35 and 36 excerpts from the Living Bible).

The Spiritual Epicentre of the World

"… The plot of land upon which the Dome of the Rock now stands is hallowed by the world's major monotheistic religions - Judiasm, Christianity, and Islam. Their conflicting claims upon the Haram Ash - Shariff, as the elevated stone platform surrounding the Dome is known, have made it the chief focus of a bitter and protracted contest of arms, one that has yet to be fully resolved. In a very real sense, old Jerusalem and the Haram stand at the spiritual epicentre of the world".('Dome of the Rock' Landay p.11)

Step Five (Dia.18)

Realizing that I had found four consecutive steps coming to an apex in 691 AD. I knew that I must project on from 691 AD by proportional time spans to the first from 38, 70, 585 and 621 years. Could it be possible that there were four more corresponding steps that would perfectly balance?

With some trepidation I added 621 years to 691 AD, and up came the figure - 1312. That year meant nothing to me, I reached for my encyclopaedia of dates and hesitantly turned the pages to 1312 AD. Was there anything there about the Temple? I scanned the list of historical events - Revolt of English barons against Edward II: execution of Piere Gaveston, Scots under Bruce invaded England: Lyons becomes part of France. There was just nothing about the Temple, Jerusalem, Palestine or even the Moslems. My heart sank in despair, I was certain the Lord was leading me to this year - but what connection did a Scotsman Robert Bruce have with the Temple - absolutely nothing!

As I was closing the book very disheartened, I noticed on the extreme right of the opposite page, a new clue still in 1312 AD, but under the science heading it stated: - "order of the Knight's Templars dissolved by Papal Decree". It was under the wrong heading, but I was heading in the right direction. The words Templars and Temple triggered some questions. Who were the Knight's Templars? What was their connection, if any, with the Temple?

I must confess my knowledge of them was almost negligible, derived mainly from Ivanhoe and the T.V. drama "The Dark Side of the Moon". I have a big well-read library of prophetic books, old and new, but none refers to the Knights Templars. So off I went again to the Reference Library. It was very hard to refrain from shouting in that silent place, when I read these words "The Knights Templars were established in 1118 AD with their headquarters in the Dome of the Rock which the Crusaders believed to be Solomon's Temple."

Praise the Lord! the TIMES OF THE TEMPLE are indeed following a symmetrical pattern! NOTE: They were actually housed in the Al-Aska Mosque on the temple site - but their spiritual headquarters was the 'Dome of the Rock'. Its octagonal design was copied in many of their temples in Europe and Great Britian.

The Knights Templars

They started with high motives, their object being to protect pilgrims worshipping at Jerusalem. Originally poor they became famous as bankers. In 1300 AD they had 15,000 members and their property included 9,000 castles and manors. The rulers of the Christian states had no control over the Knights Templars who were often at odds with other Christians, as well as with the Moslems. Some went over to Islam, and others were influenced by Moslem mystical practices.

Today, the Freemasons have inherited their name and ancient mysteries. In fact the highest order in the English structure of Freemasonry, the York Rite, is the order of Knights Templars. They were a highly secret organisation, and their prize possession was the Shroud of Turin.

St. Bernard of Clairvaux, their spiritual leader, burned publicly hundreds of dissenters at the stake and recommended malicide, the killing of the bad. ''In the death of a pagan, the Christian is glorified because Christ is glorified.'' (These excerpts from 'The Knights Templar' Stephen Howarth). In 1312 AD Pope Clement V and Philip IV of France abolished the Knights Templar.

Council of Vienne April 3rd 1312 AD

Pope Clement V :- ''We abolish the aforesaid order of the Temple, and its constitution, habit and name, by an irrevocable and perpetually valid decree; and we subject it to perpetual prohibition with the approval of the holy council, strictly forbidding anyone to presume to enter

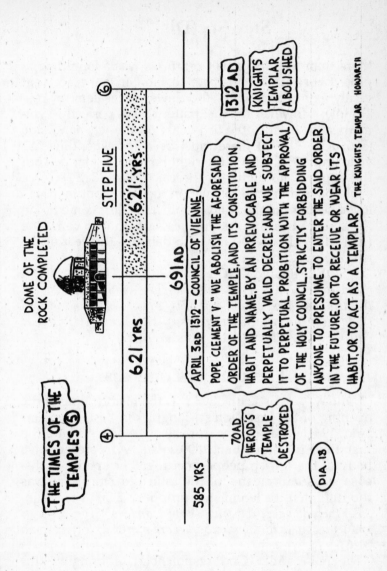

THE TIMES OF THE TEMPLES (5)

DOME OF THE ROCK COMPLETED

STEP FIVE

④ ⑥

585 YRS 621 YRS 621 YRS

70AD
HEROD'S
TEMPLE
DESTROYED

691AD

1312 AD
KNIGHT'S
TEMPLAR
ABOLISHED

APRIL 3RD 1312 - COUNCIL OF VIENNE
POPE CLEMENT V " WE ABOLISH THE AFORESAID
ORDER OF THE TEMPLE, AND ITS CONSTITUTION,
HABIT AND NAME, BY AN IRREVOCABLE AND
PERPETUALLY VALID DECREE; AND WE SUBJECT
IT TO PERPETUAL PROBITION WITH THE APPROVAL
OF THE HOLY COUNCIL, STRICTLY FORBIDDING
ANYONE TO PRESUME TO ENTER THE SAID ORDER
IN THE FUTURE, OR TO RECEIVE OR WEAR ITS
HABIT, OR TO ACT AS A TEMPLAR" THE KNIGHTS TEMPLAR HOWARTH

DIA. 18

61

the said order in the future, or to receive or wear its habit, or to act as a Templar.''

Step Six (Dia.19)

More than five and a half centuries was a long time to project forward and expect to land in an exact year vitally connected with the Jews, Jerusalem or the Temple. However, if the pattern was perfectly symmetrical to balance the 585 years on the left hand side (516 BC - 70 AD) there must be a corresponding 585 years from 1312 AD on the right hand side. I tapped out the appropriate digits on the calculator: 1312 + 585 I could have done the calculation mentally, but by now I loved seeing prophetically significant years come up on the screen. I pushed the equals sign and up came the figure 1897! I was ecstatic with delight - the year of the first Zionist Congress.

''O SOVEREIGN LORD HOW GREAT THOU ART!'' I cried in Joy ''*The Lord foils the plans of the nations; HE thwarts the purposes of the peoples. But the plans of the Lord stand firm forever, the purposes of HIS heart THROUGH ALL GENERATIONS.*''(Psalms 33: 10-11)

The Zionist Congress

''Sunday, August 29th 1897 was the historic date of the opening of the first Zionist Congress in Basle, Switzerland. 196 delegates came from all over the world, for the first time in more than 1800 years. A representative body of the Jewish people met together openly to discuss ways and means for the return to Zion. This was the fulfilment of Jeremiah's prophecy 2,500 years ago. *''For there shall be a day, that the watchman shall cry, arise ye and let us go up to Zion unto the Lord our God.''* (Jeremiah 31:6) .

The man under God responsible for bringing this Congress into being was Theodore Herzl, an Hungarian Jew, born in 1860. His princely bearing and dignified

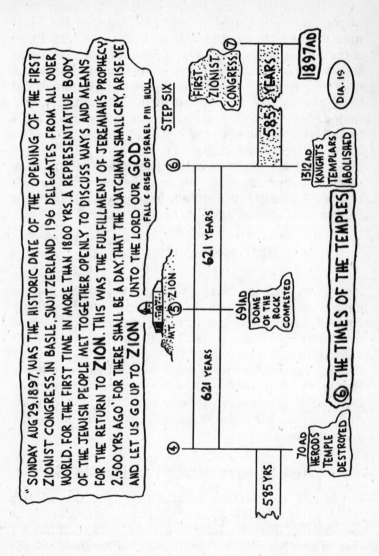

"SUNDAY AUG 29.1897, WAS THE HISTORIC DATE OF THE OPENING OF THE FIRST ZIONIST CONGRESS, IN BASLE, SWITZERLAND. 196 DELEGATES FROM ALL OVER WORLD. FOR THE FIRST TIME IN MORE THAN 1800 YRS. A REPRESENTATIVE BODY OF THE JEWISH PEOPLE MET TOGETHER OPENLY TO DISCUSS WAYS AND MEANS FOR THE RETURN TO ZION. THIS WAS THE FULFILLMENT OF JEREMIAH'S PROPHECY 2,500 YRS AGO" FOR THERE SHALL BE A DAY, THAT THE WATCHMAN SHALL CRY, ARISE YE AND LET US GO UP TO ZION UNTO THE LORD OUR GOD"

FALL & RISE OF ISRAEL P111 HULL

STEP SIX

FIRST ZIONIST CONGRESS ⑦

585 YEARS

1897AD

DIA. 15

⑥ 1312AD KNIGHTS TEMPLARS ABOLISHED

621 YEARS

MT. ⑤ ZION

691AD DOME OF THE ROCK COMPLETED

621 YEARS

④ 70AD HEROD'S TEMPLE DESTROYED

585 YRS

⑥ THE TIMES OF THE TEMPLES

63

appearance set him apart as a prophet in Israel. In his diary, Herzl recorded after this congress - "In Basle I founded the Jewish State."

On the fiftieth anniversary of this Congress at a memorial meeting held in Jerusalem, August 1947, just nine months before the State of Israel was actually to come into existence, Mr David Ben Gurion, who was soon to become the first Prime Minister said, "This was no outburst of enthusiasm on the part of a dreamer, but the expression of a profound historical institution. On that day the Jewish State was indeed founded, for a State is first founded in the hearts of the people." (The Fall and Rise of Israel Hull p.111)

This first Congress adopted the statement that the object of Zionism was "to establish for the Jewish People, a publicly recognised, legally secured home in Palestine." (The Fall and Rise of Israel Hull p.111)

Step Seven (Dia.20)

Now we can see the symmetrical pattern that is emerging. We have seen thus far steps 5 and 6 perfectly counter balancing 4 and 3. If the symmetry is to continue step 7 must match step 2 of 70 years span.

Extending 70 years from 1897 we come to the most exciting year so far in prophetic Jewish history - the Six Day war of June 1967 - when after centuries of Gentile Domination, the old city of Jerusalem, and more importantly for our study, the Wailing Wall on the Temple site was captured.

The Capture of the Wailing Wall

On June 7 1967, Israeli paratroopers took the wailing wall from the Arab legionnaires. The commander Major General Uzi Nariciss later wrote, "It was as though I was in another world...I felt a part of the whole Jewish people, who for 2,000 years had longed for this moment. It was an emotion far bigger than myself, bigger

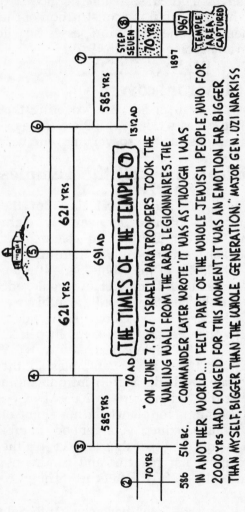

THE TIMES OF THE TEMPLE ⑦

586 516 BC.   70 AD   691 AD   1312 AD   1897   1967

70 YRS   585 YRS   621 YRS   621 YRS   585 YRS   STEP SEVEN 70 YRS   TEMPLE AREA CAPTURED

② ③ ④ ⑤ ⑥ ⑦ ⑧

"ON JUNE 7, 1967 ISRAELI PARATROOPERS TOOK THE WAILING WALL FROM THE ARAB LEGIONNAIRES. THE COMMANDER LATER WROTE 'IT WAS AS THOUGH I WAS IN ANOTHER WORLD... I FELT A PART OF THE WHOLE JEWISH PEOPLE, WHO FOR 2000 YRS HAD LONGED FOR THIS MOMENT. IT WAS AN EMOTION FAR BIGGER THAN MYSELF, BIGGER THAN THE WHOLE GENERATION." MAJOR GEN. UZI NARKISS.

THE NEXT WEEK JUNE 14, ON THE FEAST OF WEEKS 200,000 JEWS GATHERED TO PAY HOMAGE AT THE WALL.

"WE ARE AT THE STAGE WHERE DAVID WAS WHEN HE LIBERATED JERUSALEM. FROM THAT TIME UNTIL THE CONSTRUCTION OF THE TEMPLE BY SOLOMON, ONLY ONE GENERATION PASSES. SO WILL IT BE WITH US." ISRAEL ELDAD, HISTORIAN.

DIA. 20

than the whole generation." The next week, June 14, on the Feast of Weeks 200,000 Jews gathered to pay homage at the wall.

A Jewish historian Israel Eldad commented, "We are at the stage where David was, when he liberated Jerusalem. From that time until the construction of the Temple by Solomon, only one generation passes, so will it be with us." Time magazine June 30th 1967.

Step Eight (Dia.21)
(See front cover)

As we plot our final span of 38 years covering that lengthy period of 2628 years from 624 BC we come exactly, with no manipulation whatsoever, into the year 2005 AD.!

The Symmetrical Times of the Temples (Dia.22)

So here is the complete symmetrical times of the Temples - 2,628 years divided into exactly eight proportional parts, looking like a giant coat hanger (cover). When one realizes that from 1988 there are only 17 years to 2005 AD (0.64% of the whole period!) then the coat hanger becomes a cliff-hanger!! How privileged we are to be living in the last stretch of human history. The Dome of the Rock is an octagonal (eight sided) structure, (Dia.22) and here are eight steps in perfect equilibrium. Eight in the Bible speaks of a NEW BEGINNING. Just as there are seven notes in the musical diatonic scale, with the eighth introducing a new octave, so after these eight steps to 2005 AD, God introduces a new beginning for planet earth, - a time of rest and blessing for all mankind. "A larger body of prophetic scripture is devoted to the subject of the millennium, developing its character and conditions, than any other one subject." (Dr Pentecost "Things to Come" p.476)

But be warned! Only those who have come into right relationship with the living God through FAITH in the person of Jesus Christ and HIS saving work in shedding HIS blood for our Sins, will enter this era of un-

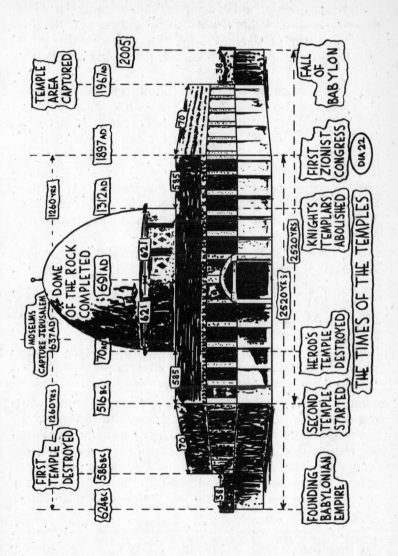

THE TIMES OF THE TEMPLES

DIA 22

Labels (top, left to right):
- TEMPLE AREA CAPTURED — 2005 / 1967 AD
- 1260 YRS — 1897 AD
- 1312 AD
- MOSLEMS CAPTURE JERUSALEM 637 AD — DOME OF THE ROCK COMPLETED 691 AD
- 821
- 70 AD
- 516 BC
- 585
- FIRST TEMPLE DESTROYED — 586 BC / 624 BC
- 1260 YRS
- 70
- 58

Labels (bottom, left to right):
- FOUNDING BABYLONIAN EMPIRE
- SECOND TEMPLE STARTED
- HEROD'S TEMPLE DESTROYED
- 2520 YRS
- 2520 YRS
- KNIGHTS TEMPLARS ABOLISHED
- FIRST ZIONIST CONGRESS
- FALL OF BABYLON

precedented joy, peace and rest (Revelation 20: 4-6). To get right with God read and act on the instructions given in Romans 10: 9-10, John 3:16 and 1:12

There is to be a period of unprecedented anguish in the preceding seven years (1999 - 2005), a thorough clean-up and sifting of all the inhabitants of this earth - but more about that period of great tribulation in later chapters.

Do you remember when we worked out the times of the Gentiles, it came to 2005 AD in solar years from 586 BC, and when we did it in prophetic years it came to 1967 AD.....? (p.45) Well, learn more of his ways, Jesus Christ - ''The Architect of the Ages''(Hebrews 1:2 literal trans.)

We have just learnt how in the TIMES OF THE TEMPLES adding 2628 solar years to 624 BC comes to 2005 AD. Now learn another incredible fact in the light of chronophecy.

If we convert 2628 solar years into prophetic years this is what happens -

$$2628 \times 360 \div 365.24 = 2590 \text{ solar years}$$
$$624 + 2590 \text{ solar years} = 1967 \text{ AD}.$$

That very, very special year when the Jews recaptured the holiest of their shrines - the Wailing Wall on the temple mound. So we have another two fold phenomenal bearing that only an Omnipotent God could organise and enact in history (Dia.23).

Eight symmetrical steps lead us to the most outstanding age of all, when Jesus Christ reigns and righteously governs planet earth. In Hebrew, the number eight is sh' moneh from the root Shah' - meign - 'to make fat' - 'cover with fat' - to 'superabound.' As a participle, it means 'one who abounds in strength' etc. So that, as a numeral, it is the super abundant number: (Number in Scripture - Bullinger p.196).

If you want to super-abound in that super-abundant age then throw in your allegiance NOW to that glorious SUPER-SON of Man - the Lord Jesus Christ, King of Kings and Lord of Lords to whom and before whom *''at*

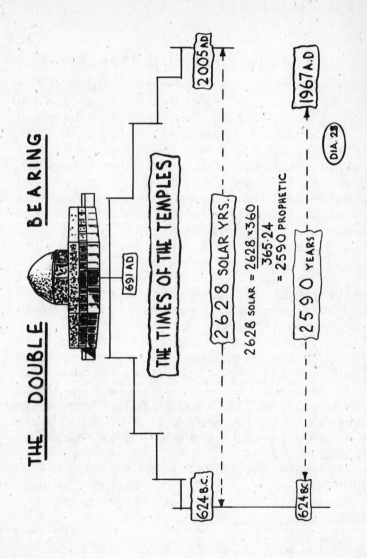

THE DOUBLE BEARING

691 AD

THE TIMES OF THE TEMPLES

624 B.C. — 2005 AD

2628 SOLAR YRS.

$$2628 \text{ SOLAR} = \frac{2628 \times 360}{365.24}$$
$$= 2590 \text{ PROPHETIC}$$

624 B.C. — 1967 A.D.

2590 YEARS

DIA. 23

the name of Jesus every knee shall bow, in heaven and on earth and under the earth, and every tongue confess that Jesus Christ is Lord, to the glory of God the Father.'' (Philippians 2:9-11; Romans 14:11).

The Rise and Fall of Babylon

The times of the TEMPLES commenced with the RISE of Babylon and ends with the FALL of Babylon (Revelation 16:19 - 18:24). 'Babel' (confusion) in the land of Babylonia, was the scene of a titanic social revolt against the RULE of God. Centuries later the city of Babylon was all of Babel and more, epitomised in stone. Babylon - religious, commercial and political, all without God, - is finally destroyed by the return of Jesus Christ, of whom it was predicted in Isaiah 9:6 - *''the government shall be on HIS shoulder.''*

Do you remember step one, when Jeremiah and others warned of the fall of Jerusalem (586 BC)? We read the recurring phrase - ''AGAIN and AGAIN,'' God warned the people through His servants the prophets - but it had little or no effect and their capital city was destroyed and they were led away into captivity.

History will repeat itself in full and final measure at the end of this age. Are you running your business without God? Does your religion lack a vital living relationship with Jesus Christ *''having a form of Godliness, but denying the power thereof.''* (2 Timothy 3:5). Do your politics acknowledge the rule and power of God? If not, take note of the repeated warnings, ''NEVER AGAIN'' in Revelation 18:21-24

''The great city of Babylon will be thrown down NEVER TO BE FOUND AGAIN''. No more trading - no more business transactions, no more shopping outings - FOREVER!

''The music of harpists and musicians, flute players and trumpeters, WILL NEVER BE HEARD IN YOU AGAIN''

No more rock concerts, no more musical recitals - no more music. Full stop, forever, to those who refuse to bow the knee to the world's new and rightful ruler.

"No workman of any trade will ever be found in you AGAIN."

No employment, no tradesman, no craftsman, no dole to all who would build on sand, (Luke 6:46-49), instead of like Abraham, *"For he was looking forward to the city whose architect and builder is God."* (Hebrews 11:10).

"The sound of a millstone will NEVER be heard in you AGAIN."

A millstone grinds wheat and barley into flour. No more FOOD - FAMINE forever to all who would live without the bread from Heaven. Jesus said, *"I am the bread of life....if a man eats of this bread he will live forever."* (John 6:48-50).

"The light of a lamp will NEVER shine in you AGAIN."

He who rejects "the light of the world" (John 9:5) will end up in gross total darkness - a judicial blindness (Isaiah 60:2; Jeremiah 13:15; Psalm 49:19) *"He will join the generation of his fathers, who will never see the light."* Donkeys working in underground mines are regularly brought to the surface otherwise they would go blind. Jesus said, *"Walk while you have the light, lest darkness come upon you."* (John 12:35). This darkness is the OUTER DARKNESS (Matthew 12:8) which will last forever! No more will you be lit up by nightclubs, drugs or massage parlours.

"The voice of bridegroom and bride will NEVER be heard in you AGAIN."

Marriage, romance, sex will never be part of your life again! But in the very next chapter, (Revelation 19) all Christians are exhorted *"Let us rejoice and be glad and give HIM glory. For the wedding of the Lamb has come and HIS bride has made herself ready. Fine linen bright and clean was given her to wear."* (v. 6-7).

WHAT COMMENTATORS SAY ABOUT THESE VERSES:-

"All of Babylon's activities - whether lucrative commerce, or opulent living or raucous pleasure - are still

71

and silent. None will ever be heard or seen any more."
(The Revelation Record. Henry Morris p.374)

"Involves crushing out the present earth system, as one would stamp out a nest of wasps...The inevitable insanity of sin which wars away in spite of defeat after defeat against God." (The Book of the Revelation. W.R. Newell)

"Suddenness, violence, and completeness are all portrayed. One moment prosperous Babylon stands a queen of cities in communication with the rest of world and is sought out by all nations. The next moment she is gone, forever gone! Mark well the words "NEVER AGAIN" and how often they are sounded in the dirge that follows.... the pride, the presumption, the perversity, of Babylon makes her the final depository of the sins of the world." (Exploring Revelation J. Phillips p.238)

If you are not a part of the BODY of Christ (1 Corinthians 12:12-27), then you are part of BABYLON - a religious, commercial, political world system that refuses to bow to the Lordship of Jesus Christ. Unless there is repentance and faith in the Son of God, then there is "NO EXCUSE" (Romans 1:20), "NO ESCAPE" (Romans 2:3), "NO DIFFERENCE" (Romans 3:22), "NO HOPE" (1 Thessalonians 4:13).

What has happened to these TEMPLES in this study will happen to you. God will overthrow every stone of your godless philosophy, and the defensive wall of a dead religion until there *"will not be left one stone upon another; everyone will be thrown down"* (Matthew 24:2).

Learn from King Zedekiah - who had been warned AGAIN and AGAIN that Babylon would destroy Jerusalem. He had been given all the light necessary to save his city, its citizens, and his own skin. But this senseless 32 year old *"Did evil in the sight of the Lord his God, and did not humble himself before Jeremiah the prophet, who spoke the word of the Lord. He also rebelled against King Nebuchadnezzar who had made him take an oath in God's name. He became stiff-necked and hardened his heart, and would not turn to the Lord, the God of Israel"*. (2 Chronicles 36:12-13).

Have you ever seen the T.V. advertisement about an attractive young lady involved in a car accident? Her numerous body injuries would heal in time, and her face with many stitches would take 18 months to recover. Then come the poignant words - "but she will be blind for the rest of her life!"

Zedekiah - the man who refused the light, lost the light! The last optical image planted on his brain and memory from his 130 million visual nerve cells was the tragic death of all his sons. *"There at Riblah the King of Babylon slaughtered the sons of Zedekiah before his eyes.....Then he put out Zedekiah's eyes, bound him with bronze shackles, and took him to Babylon, where he put him in prison till the day of his death."* (Jeremiah 52:10-11). If he lived to 70 he had 38 years to languish, reliving every day, the death of his young sons. 38 in the Bible speaks of a wasted period (Deuteronomy 2:14-15; John 5:5).

We are now more than half-way through the last time span of 38 years (Dia.21) in the times of the TEMPLES. You can either try to endure a living hell through the tribulation, or enjoy "a living hope" (1 Peter 1:3) here and now. You can wait *"for the BLESSED HOPE - the glorious appearing of our great GOD and SAVIOUR, Jesus Christ"* (Titus 2:13), or you can wait for the BLOODY HORROR, the hideous appearing of Antichrist! (2 Thessalonians 2:3-12, Revelation 13:1-18; Daniel 11:31-39) with the accompanying wrath of God. (Revelation 8:8; 9:5-6; 15;18, 16:3-4 etc, etc)

As has been well said "We can understand and forgive a child that is afraid of the dark - but it is a tragedy when an adult turns from the light."

"The god of this age has blinded the minds of unbelievers, so that they cannot see the light of the gospel of the glory of Christ, who is the image of god." (2 Corinthians 4:4).

The word 'BLINDED' comes from a Greek root meaning to burn or smoke. Just as a naval vessel puts up a smoke screen to hide from the enemy - so Satan tries to hide the facts of the Gospel from unbelievers.

Before we go any further in this thrilling study of new facts for this computer age final generation, why not

73

pray this prayer? "Dear Lord, please clear the smokescreen that is blinding and befuddling my mind. Help me to clearly discern the facts of your death, resurrection and coming again. Please send your Holy Spirit to come alongside and help, so that as the polluted smoke clears away, I may clearly discern and act on the facts you present to me - for Jesus' sake. Amen."

How marvellous is the symmetry of history as revealed in the Times of the Temples. We have seen pagan kings building or destroying on Mount Zion, where even a Moslem structure, the Dome of the Rock, occupies the central position in God's timetable. *"For God has put it into their hearts to accomplish his purpose!"* (Revelation 17:17 Daniel 5:12)

"Great and marvellous are your deeds Lord God Almighty
Just and true are your ways,
KING OF THE AGES
Who will not fear you, O Lord,
And bring glory to your name?" (Revelation 15:3-4)

"To the only God our Saviour be glory, majesty,
power and authority, through Jesus Christ our Lord,
BEFORE ALL AGES,
Now and forever! Amen (Jude 25)

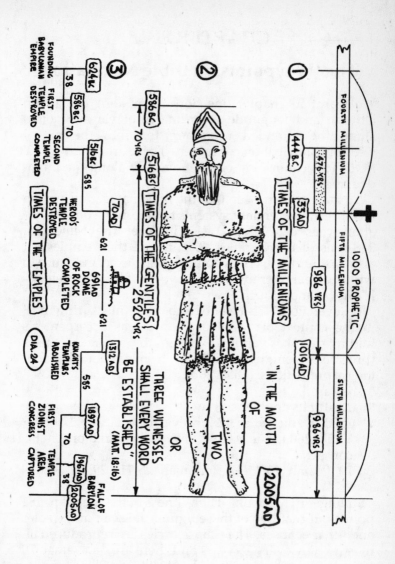

① FOURTH MILLENIUM | FIFTH MILLENIUM | SIXTH MILLENIUM

1000 PROPHETIC

444 B.C. — 476 YRS. — 33 AD — 986 YRS — 1019AD — 956 YRS — 2005 AD

TIMES OF THE MILLENIUMS

"IN THE MOUTH OF TWO"

② 586 B.C. — 70 YRS — 516 B.C.

TIMES OF THE GENTILES 2520 YRS

THREE WITNESSES SHALL BE ESTABLISHED (MATT. 18:16)

OR

③ FOUNDING BABYLONIAN EMPIRE — 624 B.C. — 38 — 586 B.C. FIRST TEMPLE DESTROYED — 70 — 516 B.C. SECOND TEMPLE COMPLETED — 585 — 70 AD HEROD'S TEMPLE DESTROYED

TIMES OF THE TEMPLES

621 — 691AD DOME OF ROCK COMPLETED — 621 — 1312 AD KNIGHTS TEMPLARS ABOLISHED — 585 — 1897 AD FIRST ZIONIST CONGRESS — 70 — 1967 AD TEMPLE AREA CAPTURED — 38 — 2005AD FALL OF BABYLON

DIA. 24

75

CHAPTER FIVE

The 'Waypoints' in Bible Navigation

We learnt in chapter one how in modern navigation latitude and longitude co-ordinates of various points along the intended route are fed into the micro-electronic navigation computer - These are called 'WAY POINTS', confirming one is travelling along the intended track.

We have already seen that the Bible navigation system has three independent systems to determine our destination year of 2005 AD (1. Times of the Millennia. 2. Times of the Gentiles. 3. Times of the Temples.) It also has numerous 'waypoints' giving exact guidance to within a year over the last 2590 years of human history - It's now almost touch down time!

In Revelation 11:1-3 we read about a "measuring rod" in the context of "1260 days". Just as a carpenter's folding ruler has varying fixed lengths, so the Bible uses three fixed lengths of time in its marvellous chronological predictions. (Dias. 26 and 27).

They are:-

1. 1260 or its double.
2. 2520 (Daniel 7:25; 12:7; Revelation 11:2-3; 12:6; 14; 13:5) 1260 in the Bible is always used in a prophetic context.
3. 70 (Isaiah 23:15-17; Jeremiah 25:11; 29:10; Daniel 9:24)

Bullinger in his book "The Witness of the Stars" p. 181 points out that two of these figures are seen in the solar and lunar eclipses. The eclipse cycles are reproduced almost exactly every 18 years and there are on average 70 eclipses in a full cycle $18 \times 70 = 1260$! (Dia.25). Truly the SUN and the MOON are for SIGNS and SEASONS (Genesis 1:14-16; Psalm 104:19).

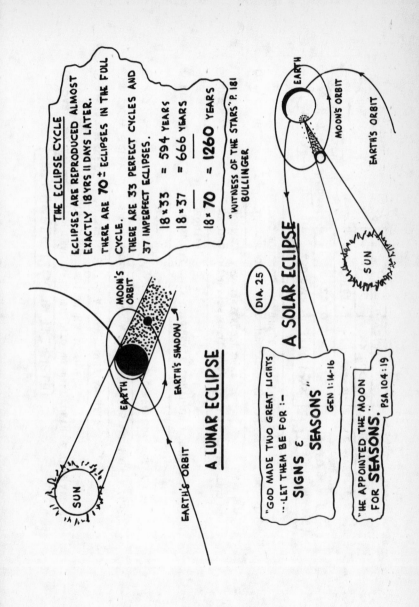

THE ECLIPSE CYCLE

ECLIPSES ARE REPRODUCED ALMOST EXACTLY 18 YRS 11 DAYS LATER.

THERE ARE 70± ECLIPSES IN THE FULL CYCLE.

THERE ARE 33 PERFECT CYCLES AND 37 IMPERFECT ECLIPSES.

$$18 \times 33 = 594 \text{ YEARS}$$
$$18 \times 37 = 666 \text{ YEARS}$$
$$\overline{18 \times 70 = 1260 \text{ YEARS}}$$

"WITNESS OF THE STARS" P. 181
BULLINGER

A LUNAR ECLIPSE

MOON'S ORBIT
EARTH'S SHADOW
EARTH'S ORBIT
SUN
EARTH

DIA. 25

A SOLAR ECLIPSE

EARTH
MOON'S ORBIT
EARTH'S ORBIT
SUN

"GOD MADE TWO GREAT LIGHTS
--LET THEM BE FOR :-
SIGNS & SEASONS"
GEN 1:14-16

"HE APPOINTED THE MOON
FOR SEASONS." PSA 104:19

77

THE NUMBER 1260 IN THE BIBLE

① DAN. 7:25. ARAMAIC "THEY SHALL BE GIVEN INTO HIS HAND UNTIL A TIME, AND TIMES AND THE DIVIDING OF TIME."

② DAN. 12:7 HEBREW "IT SHALL BE FOR A TIME, TIMES AN HALF."

③ REV. 12:14 GREEK "SHE IS NOURISHED FOR A TIME, AND TIMES, AND TIMES, AND HALF A TIME."

④ REV. 11:2 " "THE HOLY CITY SHALL THEY TREAD UNDERFOOT FORTY & TWO MONTHS."

⑤ REV. 13:5 " "POWER WAS GIVEN UNTO HIM TO CONTINUE FORTY & TWO MONTHS."

⑥ REV. 11:3 " "MY TWO WITNESSES SHALL PROPHESY A THOUSAND TWO HUNDRED AND THREESCORE DAYS"

⑦ REV. 12:6 " "AND THE WOMAN FLED INTO THE WILDERNESS... A THOUSAND TWO HUNDRED AND THREESCORE DAYS."

DIA. 26

1260 DAYS	1260 DAYS
2520 DAYS	
42 MONTHS	42 MONTHS
3½ YRS	3½ YRS
SEVEN YEARS	

DANIEL'S 70TH WEEK. 7 YRS OF 360 DAYS = 2520 DAYS

1260 IS ALWAYS USED IN A PROPHETIC CONTEXT

78

THE NUMBER 70 IN BIBLE PROPHECY

① JEREMIAH 25:11 "AND THESE NATIONS SHALL SERVE THE KING OF BABYLON SEVENTY YEARS... WHEN SEVENTY YEARS ARE ACCOMPLISHED I WILL PUNISH THE KING OF BABYLON."

② JEREMIAH 29:10 "AFTER SEVENTY YEARS BE ACCOMPLISHED AT BABYLON I WILL VISIT YOU... AND CAUSE YOU TO RETURN TO THIS PLACE."

③ ISAIAH 23:15-17 "TYRE SHALL BE FORGOTTEN SEVENTY YEARS... AFTER THE SEVENTY YEARS TYRE SHALL SING, & THE LORD WILL VISIT TYRE."

④ DANIEL 9:24 "SEVENTY WEEKS ARE DETERMINED UPON THY PEOPLE AND UPON THY HOLY CITY."

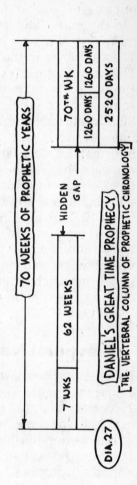

70 WEEKS OF PROPHETIC YEARS

7 WKS	62 WEEKS	HIDDEN GAP	70TH WK
			1260 DAYS | 1260 DAYS
			2520 DAYS

DANIEL'S GREAT TIME PROPHECY
[THE VERTEBRAL COLUMN OF PROPHETIC CHRONOLOGY]

DIA. 27

These fixed lengths 70, 1260 and 2520 years are used in Bible chronophecy to measure our 'WAYPOINTS'. Now to measure forwards in time, means we must be exact to the year from our starting point in history, the terminus a quo, if our terminal year, the terminus ad quem, is to be accurately known.

In the marvellous providence of God, the terminus a quo years of history in this regard are precisely known. They all range in the 500 - 700 BC time span. Professor Thiele in "The Mysterious Numbers of the Hebrew Kings" p. 161 states: "This period (500-700 BC) is in some respects the most interesting and fruitful for Biblical chronological study, for in no other period is there available such a wealth of detailed chronological information. Dates are now expressed not only in terms of years, but frequently also in terms of months and days. Frequent cross-references occur between the reigns of Hebrew and Babylonian Kings which make possible PRECISE DATING of events".

As we will be using a measuring ROD of fixed length the terminus a quo years of commencement will vary, unlike the measuring LINE used on the fixed birth years of the patriarchs (later on). So let's proceed to a very exciting aspect of this overall study of chronophecy - the 'WAYPOINTS'!

Waypoint No. One - 1897 AD (Dia.28)

Prophetic writers last century discovered this waypoint before the event. They pointed out that if one measures 2520 years from the founding of the Babylonian empire in 624 BC one comes to 1897 AD.

They were publishing before 1897 AD. We now know 1897 was the year of the first Zionist Congress - a highly important prophetic year. It is interesting to read their accurate comments. For instance, Grattan Guiness in his book 'Light for the Last Days' published in 1886 says on page 283 - "The remaining solar termination is still eleven years distant, 1897. What is it likely to witness? Some more final and fatal fall of Ottoman power? Or

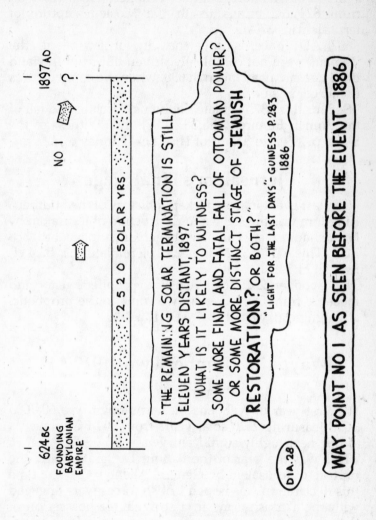

624 BC
FOUNDING
BABYLONIAN
EMPIRE

2520 SOLAR YRS.

NO 1

1897 AD
?

"THE REMAINING SOLAR TERMINATION IS STILL
ELEVEN YEARS DISTANT, 1897.
WHAT IS IT LIKELY TO WITNESS?
SOME MORE FINAL AND FATAL FALL OF OTTOMAN POWER?
OR SOME MORE DISTINCT STAGE OF JEWISH
RESTORATION? OR BOTH?"
"LIGHT FOR THE LAST DAYS" - GUINESS P.283
1886

DIA. 28

WAY POINT NO 1 AS SEEN BEFORE THE EVENT - 1886

81

some more distinct stage of Jewish restoration? Or both?'' (Dia. 28).

If we divide the 2520 years into two halves of 1260 years another interesting fact emerges - 1260 years on from 624 BC brings us to the Moslem capture of Jerusalem in 637 AD.

637 AD concerns only the city of Jerusalem, the Romans were not completely driven out from the land until Caesarea had fallen in 638, when the conquest was finally completed.

See for this 637 AD date Gibbon's 'Decline and fall of the Roman Empire' (Dia.38. p.97) and 'Witness of the Stars' p.185, also 'Dome of The Rock' Landay p.162.

Jerusalem's Final Siege

''The last event in the checkered history of the Southern Kingdom was the siege and destruction of Jerusalem by Nebuchadnezzar. This siege began on January 15th, 588 BC.'' Thiele p. 168 (2 Kings 25:1; Jeremiah 39:1; 52:4 cf, Ezekiel 24:1-2).

If we convert 2520 solar years into prophetic years, and measure from 588 BC again we come to the prophetically significant year of 1897 AD! (Dia.29).

Waypoint Number Two - 1917 AD
(Dia. 30)

The first year of Nebuchadnezzar's reign was 604/603 BC. Measuring 2520 solar years from 604 BC brings us to our next highly significant year - 1917 AD!

This was the year of the Balfour Declaration and the capture of Jerusalem by General Allenby. ''At the time this declaration was issued British forces were engaged with the Turkish army in a struggle for possession of Palestine. This document presented to the Jews something which England did not yet possess and which actually belonged to another nation...

The Balfour Declaration was the hand of God writing a

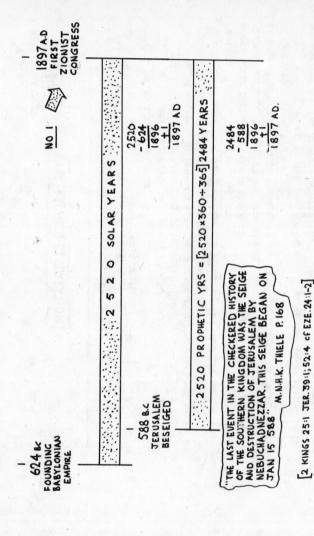

624 BC
FOUNDING
BABYLONIAN
EMPIRE

588 B.C
JERUSALEM
BESEIGED

2 5 2 0 SOLAR YEARS

2520 PROPHETIC YRS = [2520×360÷365] 2484 YEARS

NO 1

1897 A.D
FIRST
ZIONIST
CONGRESS

2520
−624
1896
+1
1897 AD

2484
−588
1896
+1
1897 AD.

"THE LAST EVENT IN THE CHECKERED HISTORY
OF THE SOUTHERN KINGDOM WAS THE SEIGE
AND DESTRUCTION OF JERUSALEM BY
NEBUCHADNEZZAR. THIS SEIGE BEGAN ON
JAN 15 588"   M.N.H.K. THIELE P. 168

[2 KINGS 25:1 JER. 39:1; 52:4 cf EZE. 24:1-2]

WAYPOINT NUMBER ONE − 1897 AD

DIA. 29

83

604 B.C.
NEBUCHADNEZZAR'S
FIRST YEAR
OF REIGN

2520 SOLAR YEARS

1917 A.D.
BALFOUR
DECLARATION

NO 2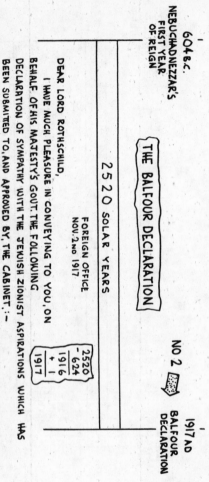

THE BALFOUR DECLARATION

FOREIGN OFFICE
NOV. 2ND 1917

2520
- 624

1896
+ 1

1917

DEAR LORD ROTHSCHILD,

I HAVE MUCH PLEASURE IN CONVEYING TO YOU, ON BEHALF OF HIS MAJESTY'S GOVT. THE FOLLOWING DECLARATION OF SYMPATHY WITH THE JEWISH ZIONIST ASPIRATIONS WHICH HAS BEEN SUBMITTED TO, AND APPROVED BY, THE CABINET.:-

"HIS MAJESTY'S GOVT. VIEW WITH FAVOUR THE ESTABLISHMENT IN PALESTINE OF A NATIONAL HOME FOR THE JEWISH PEOPLE, AND WILL USE THEIR BEST ENDEAVOURS TO FACILITATE THE ACHIEVEMENT OF THIS OBJECT. IT BEING CLEARLY UNDERSTOOD THAT NOTHING SHALL BE DONE WHICH MAY PREJUDICE THE CIVIL AND RELIGIOUS RIGHTS OF EXISTING NON-JEWISH COMMUNITIES IN PALESTINE, OR THE RIGHTS AND POLITICAL STATUS ENJOYED BY JEWS IN ANY OTHER COUNTRY."

I SHOULD BE GRATEFUL IF YOU WOULD BRING THIS DECLARATION TO THE KNOWLEDGE OF THE ZIONIST FEDERATION.

YOURS, ARTHUR JAMES BALFOUR

DIA. 30

WAYPOINT NUMBER TWO

84

warrant for his people. The same hand which wrote the law on Sinai 3,400 years earlier now wrote the confirmation of the title deed for the land He had given to Abraham. On the secular plane the Balfour Declaration was the Magna Charta of the Jewish people.''

(The Fall and Rise of Israel. Hull p. 122)

The Balfour Declaration

FOREIGN OFFICE
Nov 2nd 1917

Dear Lord Rothschild

I have much pleasure in conveying to you, on behalf of His Majesty's Government the following declaration of sympathy with the Jewish Zionist Aspirations which has been submitted to, and approved by, the cabinet:-

His Majesty's Government view with favour the establishment in Palestine of a National home for the Jewish people, and will use their best endeavours to facilitate the achievement of this object, it being clearly understood that nothing shall be done which may prejudice the civil and religious rights of existing non-Jewish communities in Palestine, or the rights and political status enjoyed by Jews in any other country!

I should be grateful if you would bring this declaration to the knowledge of the Zionist Federation.

Yours Arthur James Balfour

Seven weeks later Jerusalem, which had been held by the Turks for exactly 400 years, and for 880 years previously by the Moslems, was captured by British forces under General Allenby (Dia.31). With the events of 1897 AD and 1917 AD, one can see and sense God beginning to move in this end time pattern to converge in 2005 AD!

Another major event occurred in 1917 - the Russian Revolution on November 7th when the Communists seized power. We find Ezekiel predicting Israel's restor-

604 B.C.
NEBUCHADNEZZAR'S
FIRST YEAR
OF REIGN

|— 2520 SOLAR YEARS —|

NO 2A

1917 AD
JERUSALEM
RELEASED FROM
400 YRS OF
TURKISH RULE

"AT DAWN ON DEC. 8TH 1917 GENERAL ALLENBY ATTACKED JERUSALEM
(ALTHOUGH NOT A SINGLE SHELL FELL ON JERUSALEM ITSELF) THAT
NIGHT THE TURKS EVACUATED THE CITY. ON THE 9TH THE MAYOR OF
JERUSALEM SURRENDERED THE KEYS OF THE CITY TO GEN. SHEA,
AND DEC 11TH GENERAL ALLENBY FORMALLY, BUT HUMBLY ON FOOT,
ENTERED THE CITY AND TOOK POSSESSION."
          FOR FOUR HUNDRED YEARS JERUSALEM HAD BEEN IN TURKISH HANDS,
          AND FOR SIX HUNDRED AND SEVENTY-THREE YEARS IN MOSLEM HANDS.

"AS BIRDS FLYING, SO WILL THE LORD OF HOSTS DEFEND JERUSALEM; DEFENDING ALSO
WILL HE DELIVER IT; AND PASSING OVER HE WILL PRESERVE IT." ISA 31:5

WAYPOINT NUMBER 2A-1917   (DIA.31)

86

ation in Chaps. 36-37 and Russia's coming attack on Israel in Chaps. 38-39.

Waypoint No.3 - 1933, 1935 AD
(Dias.32 & 33)

This third waypoint points to two years, depending on whether one measures from the final siege of Jerusalem 588 BC or its overthrow and destruction in 586 BC. 2520 years added to these dates give us 1933 and 1935 AD respectively.

These two years were ominous portents for European Jews. In 1933 Hitler was appointed chancellor of Germany, the first concentration camps commenced, and there was an anti-Jewish economic boycott.

"More Jewish history was made from 1933 to 1949 than in any other epoch of which we have memory or record... within a single decade the whole international system had been totally destroyed. Fifty million people lost their lives." (Heritage. Abba Eban. p.285).

In 1935 the Nurnberg Laws were passed depriving Jews of citizen rights in Germany. All Jews were expelled from all universities. In 1935 the racist theme was given legislative expression by the enactment of the Nurnberg Laws. Jews were formally excommunicated from German society... Within a year of the adoption of the Nurnberg Laws 75,000 Jews had emigrated from Germany and 8,000 had committed suicide." (Civilization and the Jews. Abba Ebban. p.302).

The Jews had roots over 1,000 years deep in European soil and had no desire to return to their ancient homeland of Israel. So God permitted a modern Pharoah in the form of Hitler to prepare His people for Exodus II. It took a holocaust to uproot them from Europe. "From the darkest depths of man's divided nature there sprang at the throat of the Jewish people the most violent hatred that had ever convulsed the life and spirit of mankind. The agony follows us, it will never let us go... the 6 million Jews, men, women and children, carried off to

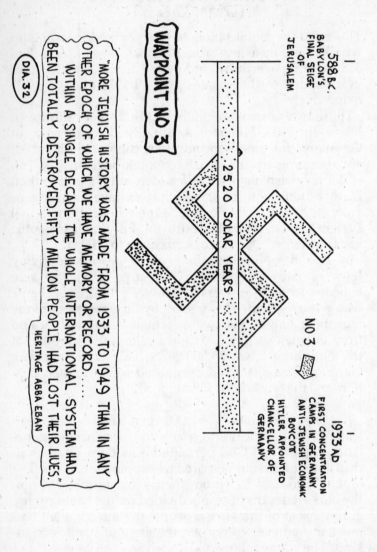

WAYPOINT NO 3

588 B.C.
BABYLON'S
FINAL SEIGE
OF
JERUSALEM

2520 SOLAR YEARS

NO 3

1933 AD
FIRST CONCENTRATION
CAMPS IN GERMANY
ANTI-JEWISH ECONOMIC
BOYCOT
HITLER APPOINTED
CHANCELLOR OF
GERMANY

"MORE JEWISH HISTORY WAS MADE FROM 1933 TO 1949 THAN IN ANY
OTHER EPOCH OF WHICH WE HAVE MEMORY OR RECORD. ....
WITHIN A SINGLE DECADE THE WHOLE INTERNATIONAL SYSTEM HAD
BEEN TOTALLY DESTROYED. FIFTY MILLION PEOPLE HAD LOST THEIR LIVES."
HERITAGE ABBA EBAN

DIA. 32

88

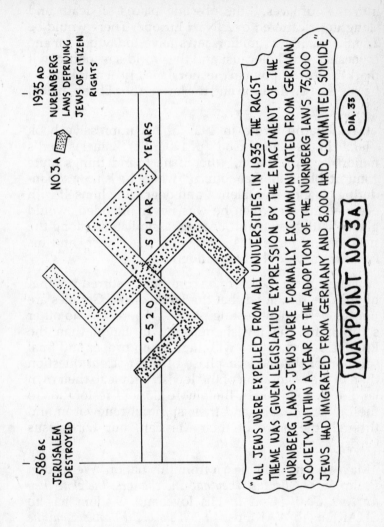

586 BC
JERUSALEM
DESTROYED

1935 AD
NUREMBERG
LAWS DEPRIVING
JEWS OF CITIZEN
RIGHTS

NO 3A

2520 SOLAR YEARS

"ALL JEWS WERE EXPELLED FROM ALL UNIVERSITIES. IN 1935 THE RACIST
THEME WAS GIVEN LEGISLATIVE EXPRESSION BY THE ENACTMENT OF THE
NÜRNBERG LAWS. JEWS WERE FORMALLY EXCOMMUNICATED FROM GERMAN
SOCIETY. WITHIN A YEAR OF THE ADOPTION OF THE NÜRNBERG LAWS 75,000
JEWS HAD IMIGRATED FROM GERMANY AND 8,000 HAD COMMITTED SUICIDE"

DIA. 33

WAYPOINT NO 3A

the gas chambers, the furnaces, the firing squads, among the one million children asphyxiated in the gas chambers in their mother's arms, or thrown still alive into the furnaces... the obscene places of death and slaughter, scattered over Nazi Europe. There would be 27 million, not 14 million Jews alive today but for the holocaust. The holocaust and the world's response to it mark the lowest point in the moral history of mankind.''

(Civilization and the Jews. Abba Ebban. p.285)

David Baron wrote in 1925 in his impressive book "Israel in the Plan of God" (p. 190 - 191) "Israel is God's national prodigal son, who, if he found things quite comfortable in the 'far country' where he is now squandering his gifts and talents, and degrading himself with occupations for which he was never intended, would gladly settle down and become assimilated among the nations and forget his sin against his Father, and his home from which he has wandered.

His nest must therefore be continually stirred up, that he may be reminded that the lands of the Gentiles are not his permanent resting place.... There was no other solution for the Jewish question in Egypt than the EXODUS, and so also will there be no proper and final solution of the modern phase of this ancient question than in the restoration of the Jewish people to their own land, to be followed by their more glorious restoration to the favour of God, and their spiritual renewal in and through the grace of their Messiah, our Lord Jesus Christ.''

May we personally learn from this nation. We read in Psalm 55:19 *"Because they have no changes, therefore they fear not God.''* God in His love and wisdom has to SHAKE us to WAKE us. *"I will shake the heavens and the earth...I will shake all nations.''* (Haggai 2:6-7)

World War One prepared the land for the Jews.
World War Two prepared the Jews for the land.

Where 19th Century Prophetic Writers Failed

The final year in 'Light for the Last Days' by Grattan Guiness (1886) is the terminal year of 1935. He came to this conclusion by adding 2520 years to the fall of Jerusalem in 586 BC (Dia.34).

Prophetic writers mistakenly thought the Times of the Gentiles covered a time span of 2520 years, when in fact, as we learnt earlier in bearing number two (Dia.10) - the Times of the Gentiles is 2520 plus 70 years = 2590 years. If they had only added 70 years to 1935 they would have come up with the year of 2005 AD (Dia.34).

Thus many Christians would not have expected the end of the age in the 1930's; nor would they have lost their faith in the phenomenal accuracy of chronophecy.

Waypoint Number Four - 1948 AD (Dias.35-36)

Nebuchadnezzar besieged Jerusalem for the first time in 606 BC. If we extend our measuring rod fully i.e. 70 + 1260 + 1260 we have 2590, the number we learnt was the Times of the Gentiles under bearing number two. If we convert 2590 solar years into prophetic years (2590 x 360 ÷ 365.24) we come up with 2553 years. Adding 2553 years to 606 BC we come to the most significant prophetic year this century - 1948 AD!! The birth of modern ISRAEL!

The budding of the fig tree (Matthew 24:32-24) in 1948-symbol of Israel's national privileges and statehood - is of course of the highest prophetic significance. We have dealt with 1948 repeatedly in other sections of this book, so will not give any more extended treatment at this stage.

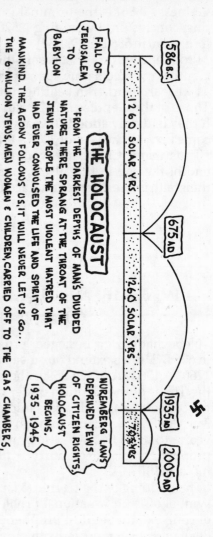

THE HOLOCAUST

FALL OF JERUSALEM TO BABYLON

586 B.C.

1260 SOLAR YRS.

675 AD

1260 SOLAR YRS.

1935 AD

70½ yrs

2005 AD

NUREMBERG LAWS DEPRIVED JEWS OF CITIZEN RIGHTS. HOLOCAUST BEGINS. 1935-1945

"FROM THE DARKEST DEPTHS OF MAN'S DIVIDED NATURE THERE SPRANG AT THE THROAT OF THE JEWISH PEOPLE THE MOST VIOLENT HATRED THAT HAD EVER CONVULSED THE LIFE AND SPIRIT OF MANKIND. THE AGONY FOLLOWS US, IT WILL NEVER LET US GO... THE 6 MILLION JEWS, MEN WOMEN & CHILDREN, CARRIED OFF TO THE GAS CHAMBERS, THE FURNACES, THE FIRING SQUADS, AMONG THE ONE MILLION CHILDREN ASPHYXIATED IN THE GAS CHAMBERS IN THEIR MOTHER'S ARMS, OR THROWN STILL ALIVE INTO THE FURNACES ... THE OBSCENE PLACES OF DEATH AND SLAUGHTER, SCATTERED OVER NAZI EUROPE."

"THERE WOULD BE 27 MILLION, NOT 14 MILLION, JEWS ALIVE TODAY BUT FOR THE HOLOCAUST."

"THE HOLOCAUST AND THE WORLD'S RESPONSE TO IT MARK THE LOWEST POINT IN THE MORAL HISTORY OF MANKIND." CIVILIZATION AND THE JEWS ABBA EBAN

DIA.34

92

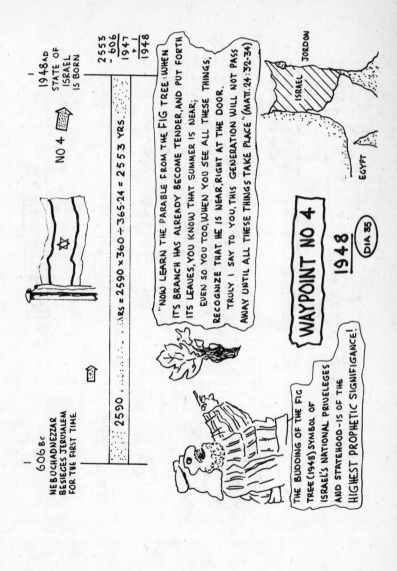

606 B.C.
NEBUCHADNEZZAR BESIEGES JERUSALEM FOR THE FIRST TIME

1948 A.D.
STATE OF ISRAEL IS BORN

NO 4

2590 .... YRS = 2590 × 360 ÷ 365·24 = 2553 YRS.

$$\begin{array}{r} 2553 \\ -606 \\ \hline 1947 \\ +1 \\ \hline 1948 \end{array}$$

"NOW LEARN THE PARABLE FROM THE FIG TREE: WHEN IT'S BRANCH HAS ALREADY BECOME TENDER, AND PUT FORTH IT'S LEAVES, YOU KNOW THAT SUMMER IS NEAR; EVEN SO YOU TOO, WHEN YOU SEE ALL THESE THINGS, RECOGNIZE THAT HE IS NEAR, RIGHT AT THE DOOR. TRULY I SAY TO YOU, THIS GENERATION WILL NOT PASS AWAY UNTIL ALL THESE THINGS TAKE PLACE" (MATT. 24:32-34)

ISRAEL   JORDON

EGYPT

WAYPOINT NO 4
1948
DIA 35

THE BUDDING OF THE FIG TREE (1948) SYMBOL OF ISRAEL'S NATIONAL PRIVELEGES AND STATEHOOD - IS OF THE HIGHEST PROPHETIC SIGNIFIGANCE!

93

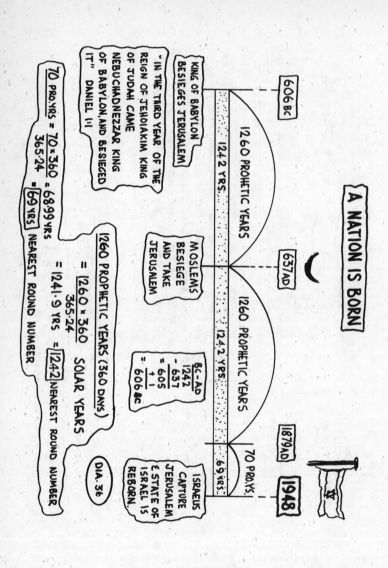

A NATION IS BORN

606 BC

1260 PROPHETIC YEARS
1242 YRS.

KING OF BABYLON BESIEGES JERUSALEM

"IN THE THIRD YEAR OF THE REIGN OF JEHOIAKIM KING OF JUDAH CAME NEBUCHADNEZZAR KING OF BABYLON, AND BESIEGED IT." DANIEL 1:1

637 AD

1260 PROPHETIC YEARS
1242 YRS.

MOSLEMS BESIEGE AND TAKE JERUSALEM

BC - AD
1242
- 637
= 605
+ 1
= 606 BC

1260 PROPHETIC YEARS (360 DAYS)

$$= \frac{1260 \times 360}{365 \cdot 24} \text{ SOLAR YEARS}$$

= 1241·9 YRS = 1242 NEAREST ROUND NUMBER

DIA. 36

1879 AD

70 PRO.YS.
69 YRS.

1948

ISRAELIS CAPTURE JERUSALEM & STATE OF ISRAEL IS REBORN.

$$70 \text{ PRO.YRS} = \frac{70 \times 360}{365 \cdot 24} = 68.99 \text{ YRS} = 69 \text{ YRS NEAREST ROUND NUMBER}$$

94

Waypoint Number Five - 1967 AD
(Dias. 37 & 38)

If we fully extend our measuring rod 1260 + 1260 + 70 solar years from the founding of the Babylonian Empire in 624 BC an amazing pattern emerges.

Our ruler of FIXED lengths fits exactly into FOUR historic dates of the utmost prophetic significance:-
1. 624 BC. Founding of Babylonian Empire
2. 637 AD. Omar captures Jerusalem
3. 1897 AD. First Zionist Congress
4. 1967 AD. Israel captures old Jerusalem and the Temple area.

As we stop and meditate on this incredible pattern that started over twenty five centuries ago and is now emerging in our time, we are surely led to pour out our hearts in praise to God for His planning and controlling world history.

"I am God and there is none like me;
  declaring the end from the beginning, and from
  ancient times things that are not yet done" (Isaiah 46:9-10).

"Jehovah of hosts hath sworn, saying, surely, as I have thought, so shall it come to pass; and as I have purposed, so shall it stand." (Isaiah 14:24).

"For the vision is yet for the appointed time, and it hasteneth toward THE END; and shall not lie; though it tarry, wait for it; because it will surely come; it will not delay" (Hab 2:3).

During that astounding Six Day War, the Jews destroyed 250 Egyptian aircraft in a 22 minute dawn raid; the Arab powers were defeated and deprived of 67,000 sq kilometres of territory; there were 689 Israelis killed, and 13,500 Arabs. On the 7th June 1967 they captured the holiest of Jewish shrines -THE WAILING WALL

Waypoint No.6 (Dias. 39-40)

Do you remember when we commenced the TIMES of

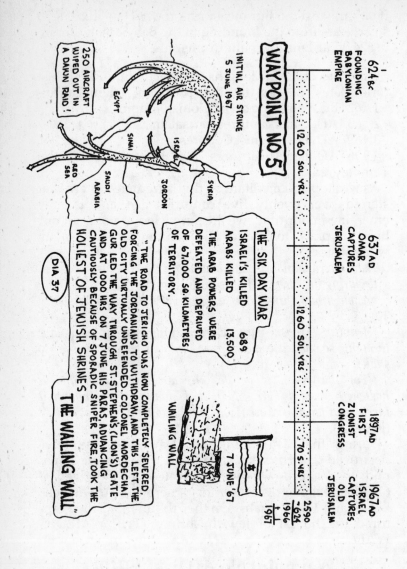

WAYPOINT NO 5

624 BC
FOUNDING
BABYLONIAN
EMPIRE

1260 SOL. YRS

637 AD
OMAR
CAPTURES
JERUSALEM

1260 SOL. YRS

1897 AD
FIRST
ZIONIST
CONGRESS

70 S. YRS

1967 AD
ISRAEL
CAPTURES
OLD
JERUSALEM

2590
−624
1966
+1
1967

INITIAL AIR STRIKE
5 JUNE 1967

EGYPT

SINAI

RED SEA

ISRAEL

JORDON

SAUDI ARABIA

SYRIA

250 AIRCRAFT
WIPED OUT IN
A DAWN RAID!

THE SIX DAY WAR

ISRAEL'S KILLED   689
ARABS KILLED   13,500

THE ARAB POWERS WERE
DEFEATED AND DEPRIVED
OF 67,000 SQ. KILOMETRES
OF TERRITORY.

"THE ROAD TO JERICHO WAS NOW COMPLETELY SEVERED,
FORCING THE JORDANIANS TO WITHDRAW, AND THIS LEFT THE
OLD CITY VIRTUALLY UNDEFENDED. COLONEL MORDECHAI
GUR LED THE WAY THROUGH ST. STEPHEN'S (LION'S) GATE
AND AT 1000 HRS ON 7 JUNE HIS PARAS, ADVANCING
CAUTIOUSLY BECAUSE OF SPORADIC SNIPER FIRE, TOOK THE
HOLIEST OF JEWISH SHRINES —

THE WAILING WALL"

WAILING WALL

7 JUNE '67

DIA 37

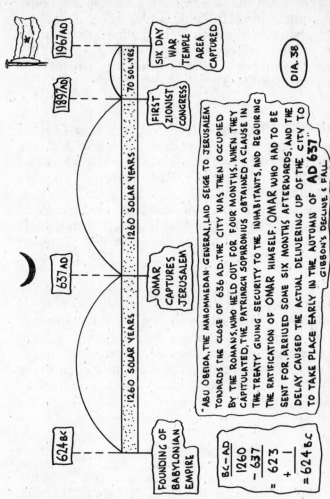

624 BC — FOUNDING OF BABYLONIAN EMPIRE

637 AD — OMAR CAPTURES JERUSALEM

1897 AD — FIRST ZIONIST CONGRESS

1967 AD — SIX DAY WAR TEMPLE AREA CAPTURED

1260 SOLAR YEARS

1260 SOLAR YEARS

70 SOL. YRS.

BC-AD
1260
− 637
= 623
+ 1
= 624 B.C

"ABU OBEIDA, THE MAHOMMEDAN GENERAL, LAID SEIGE TO JERUSALEM TOWARDS THE CLOSE OF 636 A.D. THE CITY WAS THEN OCCUPIED BY THE ROMANS, WHO HELD OUT FOR FOUR MONTHS. WHEN THEY CAPITULATED, THE PATRIARCH SOPHRONIUS OBTAINED A CLAUSE IN THE TREATY GIVING SECURITY TO THE INHABITANTS, AND REQUIRING THE RATIFICATION OF OMAR HIMSELF. OMAR WHO HAD TO BE SENT FOR, ARRIVED SOME SIX MONTHS AFTERWARDS, AND THE DELAY CAUSED THE ACTUAL DELIVERING UP OF THE CITY TO TO TAKE PLACE EARLY IN THE AUTUMN OF **AD 637**"

GIBBON'S DECLINE & FALL

DIA. 38

"637 CONCERNS ONLY THE CITY OF JERUSALEM. THE ROMANS WERE NOT COMPLETELY DRIVEN OUT FROM THE LAND UNTIL CAESAREA HAD FALLEN IN 638, WHEN THE CONQUEST WAS FINALLY COMPLETED"

97

the TEMPLES we found out (p.46) the founding of the Babylonian Empire covered the years 626/624 BC? But the pattern only unfolded correctly when we started plotting from 624 BC (see Dia.13). Likewise waypoint no. 5 plotting from 624 BC came to 1967 AD.

Now Nabopolasser's son, Nebuchadnezzar, took the throne of his father on September 7th 605 BC. (Mysterious numbers of the Hebrew Kings p.166). So this is the picture (Dia.39)

603 BC + 2520 years = 1918 AD. The year General Allenby cleared the Turks from Palestine and the Armistice for World War One was signed. If we extend our measuring rod the other fixed measure of 70 years we come to 1988 AD!

Later we will learn that Methuselah's life span plots through to 1988 (p.139) and of course it is exactly 40 years from the birth of modern Israel in 1948. Thus we have three time bearings converging into 1988. (Dia.40)

It is most likely that 1988 will see events occur in Israel of the highest prophetic significance. What will they be? We do not know. Chronophecy pinpoints the timing of events to within one year but does not forecast the actual events. However dramatic the event or events may be - it is not the END, just another waypoint on the way to 2005 AD.

Waypoint No. 7

Nebuchadnezzar captured Jerusalem on Saturday March 16th 597 BC for the SECOND time. (M.N.H. Kings p.167) extending our measuring rod out fully from 597 BC we come to 1994 AD!

Again only time will explain the events of this year in connection with Israel's forthcoming appointment with her Messiah. Converting these 2590 years to prophetic

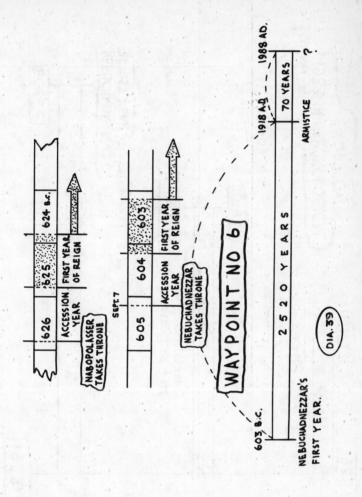

624 B.C.
625
626
ACCESSION YEAR
FIRST YEAR OF REIGN
NABOPOLASSER TAKES THRONE

SEPT 7

603
604
605
ACCESSION YEAR
FIRST YEAR OF REIGN
NEBUCHADNEZZAR TAKES THRONE

WAYPOINT NO 6

1988 A.D.
1918 A.D.
70 YEARS
ARMISTICE
2520 YEARS
603 B.C.
NEBUCHADNEZZAR'S FIRST YEAR.
?

DIA. 39

99

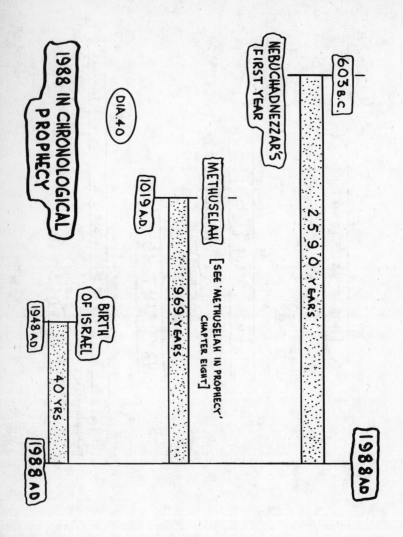

1988 IN CHRONOLOGICAL PROPHECY

DIA.40

NEBUCHADNEZZAR'S FIRST YEAR

603 B.C.

2590 YEARS

1988 AD

1019 A.D.

METHUSELAH

[SEE 'METHUSELAH IN PROPHECY' CHAPTER EIGHT]

969 YEARS

1988 AD

1948 A.D.

BIRTH OF ISRAEL

40 YRS.

1988 A.D.

$2590 \times 360 \div 365.24 = 2552.84$ years. Add these years to 597 BC and one comes to October 1956 when Israel went to war with Egypt. This was the Suez Crisis and the year Israel struck oil in the Negev.

Isaac and 2005 AD (Dia.41)

After plotting FORWARDS all the waypoints from 1897 AD (first Zionist congress) to 2005 AD, I was led by the Lord to plot BACKWARDS 1260 solar years from 586 BC (the fall of Jerusalem). How amazed I was to find it came to 1846 BC, the very year Isaac was weaned, and Jewish official time started ticking. (Dia.47). So if from 1846 BC we use all the basic measurements i.e. 1260, 70 and 2520 years (3850 years) this vast span of well over three and a half thousand years comes exactly to 2005 AD! Truly *"He has made everything beautiful in His time. He has also set eternity in the hearts of men; yet they cannot fathom what God has done from beginning to end…nothing can be added to it and nothing taken from it. God does it, so men will revere Him."* (Ecclesiastes 3:11,14)

If we convert these 3850 solar years into prophetic years, an amazingly significant prophetic fact emerges $3850 \times 360 \div 365.24 = 3794.7$ years. Adding 3794.7 years to 1846 BC comes into the year 1949 AD. Do you see the significance? For five years there had been warring in Abraham's tents between Isaac (Jew) and Ishmael (Arab) but in 1846 BC there was peace after Hagar and Ishmael departed. In 1949 the fighting that had been going on between Jew and Arab ceased when truces were declared and amnesties signed. Having concluded amnesty treaties with all her neighbouring states, Israel could now turn her attention to building up her country and caring for the thousands of immigrants that were arriving; likewise Sarah was able to give her attention to rearing her son Isaac, once Ishmael and his mother Hagar had been driven from the tents of Abraham. (Genesis 21:1-21).

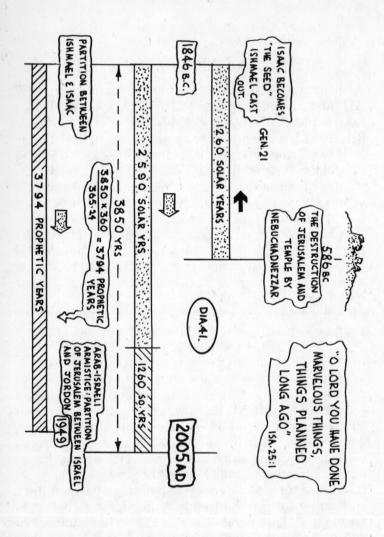

ISAAC BECOMES
"THE SEED"
ISHMAEL CAST
OUT.
GEN.21

1846 B.C.

PARTITION BETWEEN
ISHMAEL & ISAAC

3794 PROPHETIC YEARS

1260 SOLAR YEARS

2590 SOLAR YRS

3850 YRS

3850 × 360
───────── = 3794 PROPHETIC
365.24   YEARS

3794 PROPHETIC YEARS

DIA.41.

586 B.C.
THE DESTRUCTION
OF JERUSALEM AND
TEMPLE BY
NEBUCHADNEZZAR

1260 SO. YRS.

1949
ARAB-ISRAELI
ARMISTICE : PARTITION
OF JERUSALEM BETWEEN
ISRAEL AND JORDAN

2005 AD.

"O LORD YOU HAVE DONE
MARVELOUS THINGS,
THINGS PLANNED
LONG AGO"
ISA.25:1

102

"AS JESUS WAS SITTING ON THE MOUNT OF OLIVES, THE DISCIPLES CAME TO HIM PRIVATELY. 'TELL US,' THEY SAID, 'WHAT WILL BE THE SIGN OF YOUR COMING AND OF THE END OF THE AGE?'" [MAT. 24:3]

"HIS FEET SHALL STAND IN THAT DAY UPON THE MOUNT OF OLIVES" [ZECH. 14:4]

"THIS SAME JESUS, WHO HAS BEEN TAKEN FROM YOU INTO HEAVEN, WILL COME BACK IN THE SAME WAY YOU HAVE SEEN HIM GO INTO HEAVEN. THEN THEY RETURNED TO JERUSALEM FROM THE HILL CALLED THE MOUNT OF OLIVES." [ACTS 1:11-12]

1897   1917   1933   1948   1967   1988   1994

DIA. 42

GLIDE PATH

MT. OF OLIVES

THE PROPHETIC 'WAYPOINTS' TO TOUCHDOWN.

GLIDE PATH COVERS 108 YRS
= [12 × 9]   NINE IS THE NUMBER OF JUDGMENT,
"TWELVE - THE POWER OF GOD'S ADMINISTRATION AMONG MEN." DARBY

103

We can picture these 'Waypoints' as part of a glide path commencing its descent in AD 1897, and reaching its terminus in AD 2005. Thus from year of publication 1988 there are only seventeen years to touch-down! (see Dia.42).

"They will see the Son of Man coming on the clouds with power and great glory." (Matthew 24:30)

"Out of His mouth comes a sharp sword with which to strike down the nations. He will rule them with an iron sceptre. He treads the winepress of the fury of the wrath of God Almighty. On His robe and on His thigh, He has this name written - KING OF KINGS AND LORD OF LORDS" (Revelation 19:15-16).

CHAPTER SIX

The Times of Abraham, Isaac and Sarah
The Times of Abraham

Abraham was the father of the Hebrew nation. God called him out of the leading city of the world at that time - Ur of the Chaldees, and promised to his descendants:-
1. That they should inherit the land of Canaan.
2. That they should become a great nation.
3. That through them all nations should be blessed (Genesis 12:2-3; 22:18).

Thus God called Abraham to become the founder of a movement having for its object the reclamation and redemption of mankind.

On historical chronology there is a long indeterminate period between Adam and Abraham (see Appendix one), but on redemptive chronology i.e. working on revealed years, not actual years, all Bible chronologists (on Biblical data alone) are agreed that the time elapsed from the creation of Adam to Abraham's birth is a period of 2008 revealed years (Dia. 72 inside back cover).

Likewise, if we add 2008 actual years from the birth of the "Last Adam", Christ, (I Cor.15:45) in BC 4 we come once more to our terminus year, 2005 AD! (Dia. 46)

"Abraham was looking forward to the city with foundations, whose Architect and builder is God." (Hebrews 11:10). This beautiful city the "new Jerusalem" is described in Revelation chapter 21 as the dwelling place for saints of all ages, and fulfils the hope of Abraham for the heavenly city (Hebrews 11:10-16 cf. Hebrews 12:22-24).

Abraham's Birth Year

Although many dates and time spans are mentioned in the Bible, until recently it was guess work trying to tie them specifically into our calendar. Providentially in the wisdom of God the breakthrough came, when Professor Thiele of Chicago University established an absolute date for the end of Solomon's reign, and the tragic division of the nation into Judah and Israel. The key date is 931/930 BC (The Mysterious Numbers of the Hebrew Kings. pages 52-55 2nd edition).

"We may say then that the year Tishri (our mid September or mid October) 931, to Tishri 930, was the accession year of Rehoboam, and that his first official year was from Tishri 930 to Tishri 929" (p.55). If we split the difference between 931 and 929 BC we have the year 930 BC. Plotting from this datum point chronophecy comes alive (Dia.43). Thiele works from 930 BC in his new edition (p.79).

In boat building the first step is to lay down the keel to EXACT measurements. Failure to do so will throw the stern and/or the bow placement out of alignment, which will adversely affect all subsequent construction of the craft. All previous Bible chronological systems (e.g. Ussher, Panin, Anstey) lacked the establishment of an absolute date, and despite some excellent work they could not help but be out of alignment. Thanks to Professor Thiele, we can now lay down an exact keel, upon which to build an accurate chronology from Abraham to Christ.

So plotting backwards from 930 BC, the year of Solomon's death, we have our first span. *"Thus the time that Solomon reigned in Jerusalem over all Israel was forty years."* (2 Kings 11:42). Adding 40 years on to 930 we arrive at the first year of Solomon's reign 970 BC.

The next step backwards is a big leap of nearly five centuries. *"Now it came about in the four hundred and eightieth year, after the sons of Israel came out of the land of Egypt, in the fourth year of Solomon's reign over Israel....that he began to build the house of the Lord."* (1 Kings 6:1). The

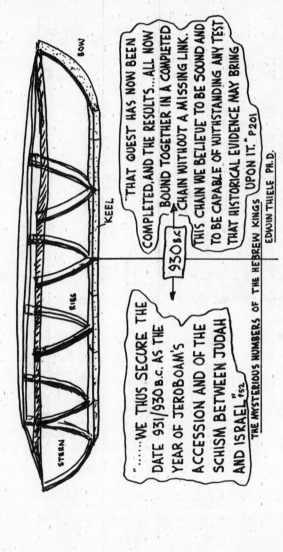

THE ESTABLISHMENT OF AN ABSOLUTE DATE IN HEBREW CHRONOLOGY.

DIA 43

SOLOMON'S REIGN

970 B.C. ←— 40 YRS —→ 930 B.C.

"THUS THE TIME THAT SOLOMON REIGNED IN JERUSALEM

OVER ALL ISRAEL

WAS **FORTY YEARS**"

(1 KINGS 11:42)

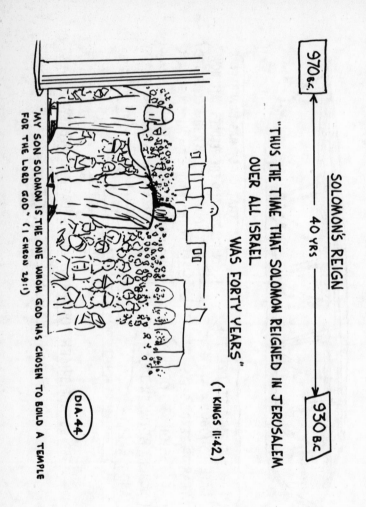

DIA·44

"MY SON SOLOMON IS THE ONE WHOM GOD HAS CHOSEN TO BUILD A TEMPLE
FOR THE LORD GOD" (1 CHRON 29:1)

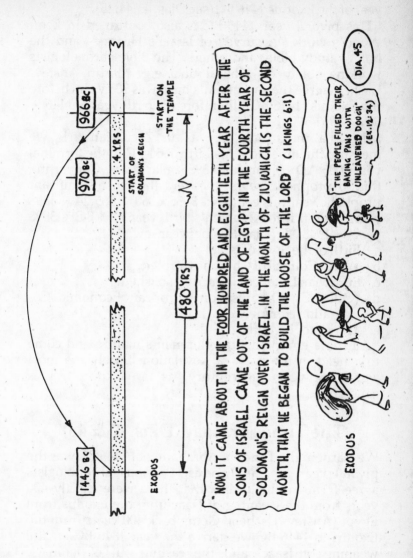

"NOW IT CAME ABOUT IN THE FOUR HUNDRED AND EIGHTIETH YEAR AFTER THE SONS OF ISRAEL CAME OUT OF THE LAND OF EGYPT, IN THE FOURTH YEAR OF SOLOMON'S REIGN OVER ISRAEL, IN THE MONTH OF ZIV, WHICH IS THE SECOND MONTH, THAT HE BEGAN TO BUILD THE HOUSE OF THE LORD" (1 KINGS 6:1)

"THE PEOPLE FILLED THEIR BAKING PANS WITH UNLEAVENED DOUGH" (Ex. 12:34)

DIA. 45

109

fourth year of Solomon's reign would be the year 966 BC (970-4). Adding these 480 years to 966 BC we come to the year of the Exodus 1446 BC (see Dias. 43,44,45).

This pivotal year 1446 BC is also confirmed in Leon Wood's work ''A survey of Israel's History'' and the N.I.V. study bible, and others. The Bible chronologists working solely on biblical data e.g. Martin Anstey, Ussher, agree that Abraham's birth was 505 years before the Exodus (1446 BC), therefore his birth year is 1446 + 505 = 1951 BC.

Using a measuring line as in Zechariah 2:1, we measure the time from his birth 1951 BC to the terminal year 2005 AD - it comes to 3955 solar years. Converting this to prophetic years uncovers the most significant prophetic year this century:- 3955 x 360 ÷ 365.24 = 3898 years. Add this to Abraham's birth year 1951 BC + 3898 years = 1948 AD (Dia.46). That year saw:

a. Birth of the State of Israel.
b. World Council of Churches formed.
c. European Defence Council established.
d. (O.E.E.C.) Organisation European Economic Co-operation commenced.
e. Transistor invented.

All these embryonic developments mature and come to a head in the book of Revelation. Surely the most significant year this century, as far as prophecy is concerned.

The Times of Isaac (Dias.47 & 48)

We learnt in the Times of Abraham that 1446 BC was the pivotal year for the Exodus. Previous chronologists agree from the Bible data that there were exactly 400 years from the weaning of Isaac until the Exodus from Egypt (Anstey, Ussher). Going back 400 years from the Exodus in 1446 BC we derive the year 1846 BC for the weaning of Isaac, and the casting out of Ishmael. (Genesis 21:1-14; 15:13; Acts 7:6; Dia. 47. See Anstey Chronology of old Testament p.58)

Abraham was the father of many nations and the

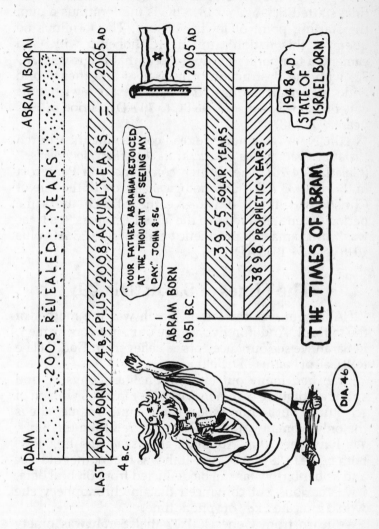

THE TIMES OF ABRAM

DIA. 46

111

FIRST JEW was Isaac, born out of a miracle (Genesis 21:5-7) and borne through time in a miraculous fashion. When Abraham obeyed God and cast out Ishmael and his Egyptian mother Hagar, the clock of official Jewish time started ticking. So 1846 BC is the terminus a quo, the starting point of Jewish history. The terminus ad quem of this nation's unique relationship with God came to a temporary abrupt stop in that tragic year AD 70, with the destruction of Jerusalem and their world wide dispersal amongst the nations. So Jewish time covers the period from 1846 BC to 70 AD a period of 1915 years. (Dia. 48)

In the New Testament we read concerning the Church *"now we, brethren, as Isaac was, are the children of promise"* (Galatians 4:28). The Church commenced at Pentecost in the year 33 AD. (Chronological aspects of the Life of Christ - Hoehner). If we give the Church the same period of time as God gave the Jews 1915 years "as Isaac was", this amazing prophetic year emerges 33 AD plus 1915 years = 1948 AD!

The Times of Sarah (Dia.49)

"If Abraham was the father, Sarah was the mother of the faithful. And if in Eve we see our ancestors as men, in Sarah we see our ancestors as believers in God." (The Roll Call of Faith; C.D. Bell)

Sarah had many outstanding qualities, physical and spiritual, that are common with other famous women of scripture - but in one aspect she is quite unique; she is the only woman whose AGE is referred to in the Bible. We have seen that Abraham and Isaac (the first Jew) both point to 1948 AD. As Sarah was the mother of Isaac and as her birth year can be deducted from Biblical data, I was curious but convinced that in chronophecy she would indicate a key prophetic time.

We learn from Genesis 17:17 that Sarah was ninety years of age at the birth of Isaac. We have already seen that Isaac was weaned in 1846 BC. As Anstey states:- "Isaac became the sole HEIR (with which we may con-

112

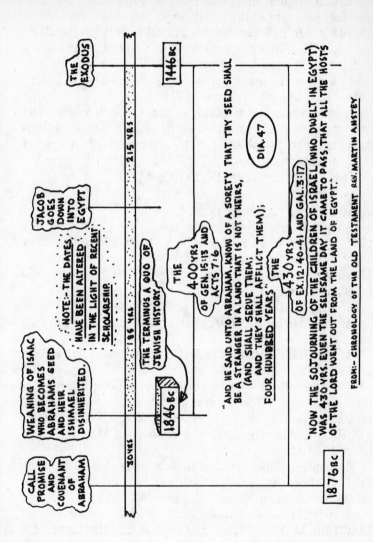

THE EXODUS

1446 BC

215 YRS

JACOB GOES DOWN INTO EGYPT

NOTE:— THE DATES HAVE BEEN ALTERED IN THE LIGHT OF RECENT SCHOLARSHIP

195 YRS

THE TERMINUS A QUO OF JEWISH HISTORY

THE 400 YRS OF GEN. 15:13 AND ACTS 7:6

"AND HE SAID UNTO ABRAHAM, KNOW OF A SURETY THAT THY SEED SHALL BE A STRANGER IN A LAND THAT IS NOT THEIRS, (AND SHALL SERVE THEM; AND THEY SHALL AFFLICT THEM); FOUR HUNDRED YEARS."

DIA. 47

WEANING OF ISAAC WHO BECOMES ABRAHAMS SEED AND HEIR. ISHMAEL DISINHERITED.

1846 BC

THE 430 YRS OF EX. 12:40-41 AND GAL. 3:17

"NOW THE SOJOURNING OF THE CHILDREN OF ISRAEL (WHO DWELT IN EGYPT) WAS 430 YRS. EVEN THE SELFSAME DAY IT CAME TO PASS, THAT ALL THE HOSTS OF THE LORD WENT OUT FROM THE LAND OF EGYPT."

FROM:— CHRONOLOGY OF THE OLD TESTAMENT REV. MARTIN ANSTEY

CALL PROMISE AND COVENANT OF ABRAHAM

30 YRS

1876 BC

113

nect the word SEED) of Abraham on the day that he was weaned, he was then five years old. On that day Abraham made him a great feast, to celebrate the event. Ishmael was Abraham's heir no longer. Isaac had taken his place. He mocked, and was cast out. (Genesis 21:8-10)''.... (The Chronology of the Old Testament, p.60).

So the birth of Isaac is simply 1846 BC + 5 = 1851 BC.

As Sarah was ninety years of age at his birth, her birth year is 1851 BC + 90 years = 1941 BC.

We have seen that measuring from a birth year of the patriarchs to the terminus ad quem 2005 AD, and then converting to prophetic years - always yields a year of tremendous significance.

The time span from 1941 BC to 2005 AD
= 3945 years

Converting to prophetic years
$3945 \times 360 \div 365.24 = 3888.4$ years
$1941 + 3888.4 = 1948.4$ AD = May 1948, the very MONTH modern Israel was born!

Three times we read that Isaac was to be born at a SPECIFIC time:-

"At this SET TIME in the next year" (Genesis 17:21)

"At the TIME APPOINTED I will return" (Genesis 18:14)

"At the SET TIME of which God has spoken" (Genesis 21:2 KJV).

How marvellous that Isaac should be born at an exact BIOLOGICAL TIME to commence the Jewish nation, and at the same time be born in CHRONOPROPHETIC TIME to indicate exactly the rebirth of the nation in MAY 1948 AD.

"Remember, I am God, and there is none else;... declaring the END from the BEGINNING, and from ancient times the things that are not yet done." (Isaac 46:9-10 KJV).

It is most interesting that Christ ascended to heaven on May 14th 33 AD (Hoehner). On that day the last recorded words of the disciples to Christ were *"Lord wilt thou at this time, restore again the Kingdom to Israel?"* (Acts 1:6). On the very same day 1915 years later, May 14th 1948 AD the State of Israel came back into existence!

114

The Battle for Israel

May 1948 saw the Israelis being attacked on three fronts by Arab armies from Lebanon, Iraq, Syria, Jordan and Egypt, numbering approximately 37,000 troops. The Israeli Defence Force (I.D.F.) had only a field force of 28,000 troops, ill-equipped and relatively inexperienced. The scene appeared to be set for an Israeli tragedy. But Jewish bravery, resourcefulness, determination and God's help, enabled them to win a notable victory in the nine months war from May 1948 to January 1949.

David Ben Gurion, Israel's first Prime Minister, announced the birth of the State of Israel in these words:-

"With trust in the Almighty,....in the city of Tel Aviv, on the 5th day of IYAR 5708, the 14th day of May 1948, let us stand to adopt the scroll of the establishment of the Jewish State". Ezekiel 36:24 had become a reality! - *"For I will take you from among the heathen, and gather you out of all countries, and will bring you into your OWN LAND."*

Since 1948 Israel and the Church have been moving to their respective destinies, Israel to meet the Son of Man on the Mt of Olives (Zech 14:4), the Church to meet the Son of God at her appointed rendezvous in the AIR (1 Thessalonians 4:16-18). *"EVEN SO, COME LORD JESUS"* (Revelation 20:20).

The other incredible chronophecy concerning Isaac, covering a span of 3850 years which converges into 2005 AD, was explained under the section on "Way" points (p. 101.) Thus both Abraham and Isaac doubly point to 1948 and 2005 AD.

"Have you not heard?
Long ago I ordained it,
In days of old I planned it;
Now I have brought it to pass" (2 Kings 19:25).

"O that men would praise the Lord for
His wonderful works to the children of men" (Psalm 107:8).

115

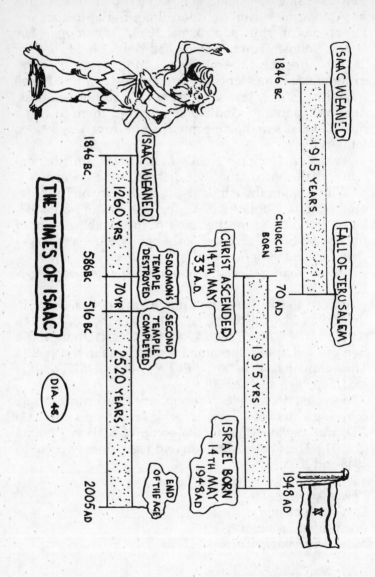

THE TIMES OF ISAAC

DIA. 48

ISAAC WEANED — 1915 YEARS — FALL OF JERUSALEM
1846 BC — CHURCH BORN — 70 AD

ISAAC WEANED
1846 BC. — 1260 YRS. — 586 BC — 70 YR — 516 BC

SOLOMON'S TEMPLE DESTROYED
SECOND TEMPLE COMPLETED

CHRIST ASCENDED 14TH MAY 33 A.D.

1915 YRS

2520 YEARS

ISRAEL BORN 14TH MAY 1948 A.D.
1948 AD

END OF THE AGE
2005 AD

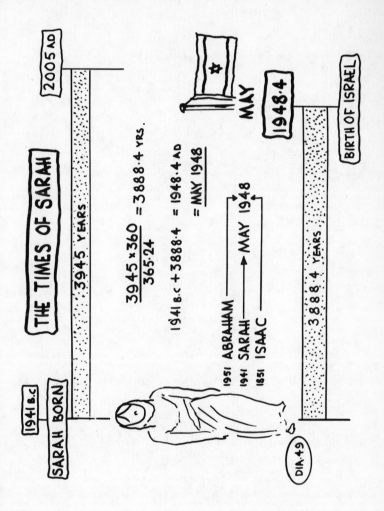

THE TIMES OF SARAH

2005 AD

1941 B.C — SARAH BORN

3945 YEARS

$$\frac{3945 \times 360}{365 \cdot 24} = 3888 \cdot 4 \text{ YRS.}$$

1941 B.C + 3888·4 = 1948·4 AD
= MAY 1948

1951 ABRAHAM
1941 SARAH → MAY 1948
1851 ISAAC

MAY
1948·4

BIRTH OF ISRAEL

3888·4 YEARS

DIA. 49

CHAPTER SEVEN

The Times of Jacob, Joseph and Moses
The Times of Jacob (Dia.50)

Of all the patriarchs Jacob is predominently the one associated with future terror and trouble for Israel.

"Cries of fear are heard - terror not peace... How awful that day will be! None will be like it. It will be a time of trouble for Jacob" (Jeremiah 30:4-7).

"There will be a time of distress such as has not happened from the beginning of nations until then." (Daniel 12:1).

"For then there will be great distress, unequalled from the beginning of the world until now - and never to be equalled again. If those days had not been cut short, no one would survive." (Matthew 24:21-22).

We have already seen how Abraham and Isaac point to the significant years 1948 and 2005 AD - so we also should expect Jacob to point to a vital prophetic year. This trio of patriarchs are invariably linked together.

"The God of Abraham, Isaac and Jacob" (Exodus 3:16).

"Your fathers Abraham, Isaac and Jacob" (Deut. 1:8).

"His covenant with Abraham, Isaac and Jacob" (2 Kings 13:23).

So we can confidently investigate Jacob's birth year and see if it does indeed link up with a prophetic year for Israel. According to Anstey and other chronologists Jacob was born 160 years after Abraham's birth, which was 1951 BC. Subtracting 160 years we come to 1791 BC for the birth of Jacob.

The last 3.5 years of the final seven years of man's government of this planet i.e. 2002-2005 is known specifically as "The Great Tribulation". "The Time of Jacob's Trouble" measuring from his birth in 1791 BC to the beginning of the Great Tribulation 2002 AD we have a period of 3792 solar years. Converting to prophetic, 3792 x 360 ÷ 365.24 = 3737 years. Adding 3737 years to 1791 BC brings us to 1947 the very year the U.N.O. General Assembly voted to grant part of Palestine to Israel!

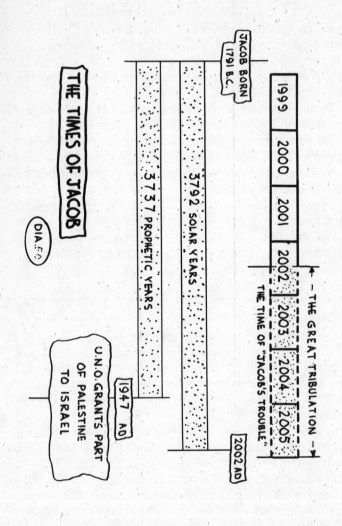

THE TIMES OF JACOB

DIA. 50

See 'The Times of Joseph' for details of this historic event.

Abraham and his son Isaac point to 1948; Jacob and his son Joseph, as we will learn next, point to 1947! What an amazing book is the Bible! The reason people are down on the Bible, is because they are not up on it!

The Times of Joseph (Dias.51-52)

As one drives towards a mountain one often cannot see it directly, but there reflected in the lake miles away is a beautiful picture of the mountain.

Joseph is the clearest reflection of Christ we have in the Old Testament. For example note how these details of Joseph's life parallel the life and work of Christ:-

1. He was loved by his father (Gen 37:3 cf John 15:9).
2. Hated by his brethren (Gen 37:4 cf John 15:23-25).
3. Sold for pieces of silver (Gen 37:28 cf Matthew 26:15).
4. Numbered with the prisoners (Genesis 39:20 cf Mark 15:27)
5. The apparent culprit between two offenders of whom one is exalted, the other perishes (Genesis 41:13 cf Luke 23:39-43).
6. Raised from prison to the right hand of majesty (Genesis 41:41-44 cf Philippians 2:9-11).
5. Recognised by his brethren as the one they sought to kill (Genesis 45:4 cf Zechariah 12:10).

There are of course many more details - but these show clearly that Joseph is a very clear picture of Christ. Like Moses, Joseph is involved with the Hebrews during their time in Egypt. For the purpose of this study the key point is when Joseph had just made himself known to his brothers - and they were fearful of the consequences, then Joseph said to them,

"It was to save lives that God sent me ahead of you. For two years now there has been famine in the land, and for the next five years there will not be ploughing or reaping. But God sent me ahead of you to preserve for you a remnant on earth and to save your lives by a great deliverance." (Genesis 45:5-7).

These two plus five years are a reflection of the actuality of the Tribulation Period (Dia.51).

As Joseph shows himself to only ten Hebrews at first and later all the Hebrews, seventy meet him in Egypt (Exodus 1:5). So early in the Tribulation 144,00 from all the tribes of Israel are sealed as servants of God (Revelation 7:3-8), but at the end of the Tribulation all Israel meets the Lord as He gathers them worldwide. (Ezekiel 37:21-22; Jeremiah 31:8-10 etc).

So two years into the tribulation as, in Genesis 45:6, gives us our terminal year for our calculation 2001 AD. As with Abraham, Isaac and Moses we start with the birth year of Joseph. As we learnt earlier Moses was born 1526 BC and according to Anstey etc. Joseph was born 174 years before Moses. Therefore Joseph was born 1526 + 174 = 1700 BC.

Measuring the time from 1700 BC to 2001 AD we have 3700 solar years. As we have seen several times earlier, changing solar years into prophetic years uncovers a very significant year in prophecy $3700 \times 360 \div 365 \times 24 = 3646.91$ years (Dia.51) 1700BC + 3646.91 = Nov 1947.

What a momentous time for Israel was November 1947! The United Nations Organisation General Assembly met November 26th to grant part of Palestine to Israel.

''For the first time in the history of the U.N.O. Russia and the U.S.A. were able jointly to support a major decision - the final decision was postponed to Saturday, the Jewish Sabbath 29th November. Did it signify that peace and rest were finally to come to Israel, and bring to an end their homelessness and nearly 2000 years of wandering in Gentile lands? Was the wandering Jew to have a home at last?

One delegate after another rose to speak. The Arabs sought to introduce a motion of postponement, but the U.S.A. and Russia quickly neutralized their arguments. It almost seemed that God had intervened for one brief moment between the great powers of the Western and Eastern world. The event was of tremendous significance. The Rabbis in Jerusalem addressed an appeal to

THE TIMES OF JOSEPH

"FOR TWO YEARS NOW THERE HAS BEEN FAMINE IN THE LAND, AND FOR THE NEXT FIVE YEARS THERE WILL NOT BE PLOWING AND REAPING. BUT GOD SENT ME AHEAD OF YOU TO PRESERVE FOR YOU A REMNANT ON EARTH AND TO SAVE YOUR LIVES BY A GREAT DELIVERANCE" [GEN. 45:6-7]

| 1999 | 2000 | 2001 | 2002 | 2003 | 2004 | 2005 |

JOSEPH MAKES HIMSELF KNOWN TO HIS BRETHEREN

JOSEPH BORN 1700 B.C.

3700 SOLAR YEARS

3646·91 PROPHETIC YEARS

2001 AD
DIA.51
NOV 1947 AD

"FOR THE FIRST TIME IN THE HISTORY OF U.N.O. RUSSIA AND THE UNITED STATES WERE ABLE JOINTLY TO SUPPORT A MAJOR DECISION. ... THE MOTION HAD RECEIVED A TWO THIRDS MAJORITY. A JEWISH STATE WAS TO ARISE AFTER MORE THAN TWENTY CENTURIES OF TIME. IT WAS V-DAY FOR ISRAEL. GOD WAS FURTHER VINDICATING HIS WORD AND PREPARING ISRAEL FOR ITS FINAL EXALTATION" LAKE SUCCESS "NOV. 29 (HULL)

123

the nations of all faiths.

At this great historic moment, when the future of Israel is hanging in the balance, we appeal to all the nations - Christians, Islamic and other - to perceive the hand of Divine Providence which has preserved Israel in almost miraculous fashion to the present day for some great world purpose, and to appropriate the eternal significance of the task now laid upon them.

Let your decision shine forth in the light of day to restore to Israel, a homeless wanderer for the past 2000 years, His Holy land for His own salvation and redemption, for the good of all who dwell in it, regardless of race and creed, and the spiritual and moral good of the whole of humanity.

The chief Rabbinate issued an appeal to the Jewish community to pray at the Wailing Wall for a favourable decision of the United Nations.

At last, just as dusk was about to bring the Sabbath Day to a close, the voting began. One Nation after the other registered their vote. Yes, No or Abstain. Then Dr. Aranha announced :- 33 in favour of partition, 13 against, and 11 abstentions. The motion had received the two-thirds majority required to pass a measure. Palestine was to be partitioned. A Jewish state was to arise after more than twenty centuries of time. It was V-Day for Israel. God was further vindicating His work and preparing Israel for its final exaltation." (The Fall & Rise of Israel - Hull p.282)

How marvellous that Joseph's birth pinpoints the very year and month that U.N.O. brought Israel back into a legal nation - or was it the Sovereign Lord? Marvellous that it is the correct year and month. I praise the Lord that it is the correct DAY also. The General Assembly of the United Nations Organisation met at Flushing Meadow, under the chairmanship of Dr. Oswaldo Aranah, on Wednesday November 26th 1947. On the 29th November l947 U.N.O voted Israel a nation once more.

Follow me as we do this simple calculation (Dia.52):-

3700 x 360 ÷ 365.24 = 3646.91 years, from Joseph's birth (1700 BC) add 3646.91 years and it equals 1947.91 AD. To find what .91 of a year is in days we simply multiply 365.24 x .91 = 332.36 days. Subtracting 332.36 days from 365.24 days equals 32.8 days (33 nearest full day). Counting back 33 days from December 31st brings us exactly to the 29th November!! The very day the General Assembly voted a nation into existence - Israel!

How God delights to work to the very day; for example,

"Now the length of time the Israelite people lived in Egypt was 430 years. At the end of the 430 years, to the VERY DAY, all the Lord's divisions left Egypt" (Exodus 12:40-41)

"God hath determined the TIMES before appointed of all nations of men. He Himself fixed beforehand the EXACT times." (Acts 17:26 Good News Bible). How fitting that Joseph, the most perfect reflection of Christ in the Old Testament, should provide the most exact calculation to the very day! Joseph brought his starving Hebrew family into a land of plenty. In November 1947 he appears again in mathematical form to provide a land for the emaciated starving Jews of Europe - O God how great thou art!

"Have you not heard? Long ago I ordained it. In days of old I planned it; Now I have brought it to pass." (2 Kings 19:25). *"Great is our Lord and mighty in power."* (Psalm 147.5).

The Times of Moses (Dia. 53)

In Alva McClain's excellent book "The Greatness of the Kingdom" we read:-

"There is a definite parallel between the supernatural preparation for the Kingdom in history under Moses and the supernatural judgments which shall be poured out upon a rebellious world in preparation for the future millennial kingdom of our Lord Jesus Christ at His second advent. There is the same insolent challenge to the true God on the part of the Gentile powers (Psalm 2:1-3). There will be a similar gracious but infinitely

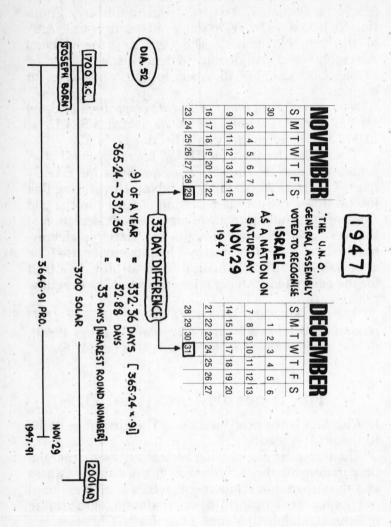

DIA. 52

1947

NOVEMBER

S	M	T	W	T	F	S
30						1
2	3	4	5	6	7	8
9	10	11	12	13	14	15
16	17	18	19	20	21	22
23	24	25	26	27	28	29

THE U.N.O.
GENERAL ASSEMBLY
VOTED TO RECOGNISE
ISRAEL
AS A NATION ON
SATURDAY
NOV. 29
1947

DECEMBER

S	M	T	W	T	F	S
	1	2	3	4	5	6
7	8	9	10	11	12	13
14	15	16	17	18	19	20
21	22	23	24	25	26	27
28	29	30	31			

33 DAY DIFFERENCE

·91 OF A YEAR = 332·36 DAYS [365·24 × ·91]
365·24 − 332·36 " 32·88 DAYS
" 33 DAYS [NEAREST ROUND NUMBER]

JOSEPH BORN

1700 B.C.

3646·91 PRO.

3700 SOLAR

NOV. 29
1947·91

2001 AD

126

greater preliminary miracle - the Rapture of the Church - warning men of the supremacy of Jehovah and the ultimate defeat of all who rebel against Him. There will be the same swift progression in the severity of the divine judgments which follow, and even a striking parallel in the nature of the judgments (cf Rev 6 through 18). There will be the same victorious outcome, the destruction of the Antichrist and his armies in the judgment of Armageddon, and the deliverance of the people of Israel (Revelation 19). There will be another song of victory, significantly referred to as the *'song of Moses.....and the song of the Lamb''* (Revelation 15:1-3).

We read in Revelation 11:1 - *''I was given a reed like a measuring rod, and was told go and measure the temple of God and the altar.''* In Zechariah 2:1 we read ''There before me was a man with a measuring line in his hand.'' God uses two measures, one of fixed length - a measuring rod, and a variable length like a builder's tape measure. Let us measure from the birth of Moses to the beginning of the Tribulation in 1999 AD with which he is strongly associated - in fact many prophetic writers believe he is one of the two WITNESSES (Revelation 11:1-13).

We have shown that the Exodus occurred in 1446 BC. Now as Moses was eighty years old at the time of the Exodus (Exodus 8:6) the year of his birth is 1446 + 80 = 1526 BC. Now with our tape measure we find that the time span from 1526 BC through to 1999 AD covers a period of 3524 solar years.

We have shown in previous chapters that converting solar years into prophetic years uncovers a hidden, very significant year in prophecy. So let us convert our time span of 3524 solar years into prophetic years thus:-

$$3524 \times 360 \div 365.24 = 3473 \text{ years}$$

Adding 3473 years to 1526 BC we come to that incredible year in prophecy 1948 AD! (Dia.53).

Moses' name means ''to draw out'' (Exodus 2:10). In fact Moses' name in Hebrew sounds like the Hebrew for draw out. As he was rescued by a Gentile, the Egyptian Princess from the waters of the Nile, so Israel in 1948 was drawn out of the waters of the nations (waters signifies nations, Revelation 17:15) by the action of the Gentiles in a majority vote of U.N.O. As Pharaoh had given the order that every Hebrew boy should be drowned in the river (Exodus 1:22) but Moses was providentially 'drawn out' from that disastrous decree, so a modern Pharaoh, Hitler, decreed the death of all Jews, but out of the Holocaust the Israeli nation like Moses was lifted out of the Gentile waters by Gentiles. In 1948 Jews returned home from more than 80 nations - from 14th May to the end of 1948 they were crossing the borders into Israel on average one every five minutes!

Moses taken out of the waters as a helpless babe is also a picture of helpless and hopeless sinners taken out of the waters of this world. At the first ever Church Council James declares:-

"God at the first did visit the Gentiles, to TAKE OUT of them a people for His name." (Acts 15:14).

This is the primary objective in God's program for this age. In 1 Corinthians Paul refers to the Jews, the Gentiles and the Church of God. The Church is the ekklesia (Greek) - the "called out assembly." The gospel has never anywhere converted all, but everywhere has called out some. No mention is made in this passage of gathering out the remnants from Israel in this age (Romans 11:5) because this was not the issue in dispute at the Jerusalem Council. *"After this* (i.e. the out-calling) *I will return."* James quotes from Amos 9:11-12. The verses which follow in Amos describe the final regathering of Israel. In connection with this purpose of "calling out" these words of Harry Lacey dealing with the social gospel are most relevant. It is an extended quotation as many sincere Christians are labouring under the misapprehension that it is their task to set up the Kingdom now!

The Inadequacy of Christian Ethics

"The line of demarcation between the world and the Church was more distinct in the first century than today. Then the Church and the Empire were separate.

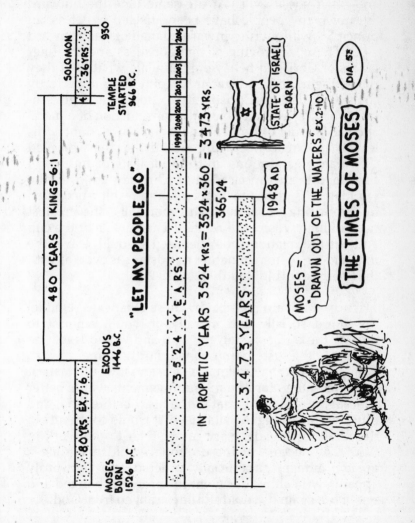

MOSES BORN 1526 B.C.

80 YRS. EX.7:6

EXODUS 1446 B.C.

480 YEARS   I KINGS 6:1

TEMPLE STARTED 966 B.C.

SOLOMON   36 YRS.   950

"LET MY PEOPLE GO"

3 5 2 4   Y E A R S

IN PROPHETIC YEARS 3524 YRS = $\frac{3524 \times 360}{365 \cdot 24}$ = 3473 YRS.

1999 2000 2001 2002 2003 2004 2005

STATE OF ISRAEL BORN

1948 AD

3 4 7 3   YEARS

MOSES = "DRAWN OUT OF THE WATERS" EX.2:10

THE TIMES OF MOSES

DIA. 5ᴱ

But now many organisations which claim to be Christian, feeling a responsibility to deal with social problems, have become interested in, and in some cases associated with politics, in the hope of eliminating war and other social evils. At the same time the outward lives of many people have been affected by Christian principles without any inward change of heart toward God. These, approving of righteousness and the finer graces of Christian behaviour, emulate what little they can of them, and endeavour to apply their imperfectly conceived ideas of Christianity to politics and government, having as their object the introduction of a moral and social order of righteousness and peace. But all this leaves the real need untouched. If the so-called Christian organisations and the idealists of the world combined in the application of Christian ethics to the world and its governments, and, as a result, succeeded in eliminating social evils and moral ills, the greatest need of man would still remain. The outside of the cup and of the platter thus cleansed, would leave the inherent sin of human nature as existent as ever (as with the Pharisees of old, Matthew 23:25-28).

Hence, if it were possible by these means, to remodel the world socially and morally, it would amount to healing the outbreaks on the skin and would leave the disease in the system untouched. Furthermore, though it might make the world more pleasant, it would make it more deceiving, for its very improvements would better conceal the real need, that of the heart before God, and thus, by concealing the vital need, it would contribute to the work of the adversary rather than to the work of God. The success of these efforts would make life a greater mirage, superficially ordered and outwardly apparently healthy, but men, inwardly unchanged and not "born again", would still be estranged from God.

After all, the very evils of the world are a blessing, for the existence of these evils emphasises that to which most close their eyes - that things are not right, and that this is so because men are not right in heart with God...Man's real need is of Christ, not the teachings of Christ, not the ethics of Christ. His need is the Christ as a Person, and as a Person who is Saviour because of His sacrifice and atonement for men.

It follows, therefore, that the work of the Church is not a moral work, nor a social work, but a spiritual one, a work which goes to the root of men's need with a message that presents Christ as a living Saviour and Lord to be personally received. The power of this message of the Gospel has millions of times met the need of earth's most wretched sinners and reconciled them to God; and they have gone on to live changed lives which demonstrate that correct morals and proper social behaviour are the fruit of the heart being right with God.

"The application of Christianity to social and moral needs without individual conversion is not only subversive of the Gospel, but is impractical, because of the corruption of the human heart." (God and the Nations 2nd Edition. Harry Lacey p. 116-118).

"This simple Gospel that brings peace with God into individual hearts is the only hope for peace among the nations; yet many well-meaning Christians have relegated it to second place in their zeal to join in activist programs to promote world peace - something unknown to Christ or the Apostles. Social activism has become "the larger mission of the church" and is expected to bring peace, love and brotherhood to a world that is still at war with God. It is like offering an aspirin when open heart surgery is required." (Beyond Seduction. Dave Hunt p.248).

"This concern about the social and political conditions, and about the happiness of the individual and so on, has always been dealt with most effectively when you had reformation and revival and true preaching in the Christian church. I would go further and suggest that it is the Christian church that has made the greatest contribution throughout the centuries to the solution of these very problems...the hospitals originally came

131

through the church...the same is true of poor re-
lief...your trade unions and other such movements, you
will find, if you go back to their beginnings, have almost
invariably had Christian origins.'' (Preaching and
Preachers. D. Martyn Lloyd-Jones p.36).

Dear Christian reader as the end of this age is fast
closing IN, are you busy drawing OUT? Winning others
to Jesus Christ? Moses, as the adopted son of Pharaoh's
daughter had a good chance of becoming Egypt's King -
but he turned down influential power. As King, he
could have abolished slavery, and restored the Jews to
their former position of splendour, as enjoyed under
Joseph. But he would not have delivered them out of
Egypt. The social gospel only improves present state,
but does not affect future standing.

CHAPTER EIGHT

The Days before the Flood
"As it was....so will it be"
(Matthew 24:37)

In Matthew 24:37-39 our Lord taught that the end time prior to His return would parallel the "days of Noah" and the "days before the flood." The record in Genesis six reads like a modern newspaper with its reference to:-
a) Population increase v.1.
b) Perverted sex v.2 & 4.
c) Wickedness v.5, violence 11-13, corruption 11-12.

The social and spiritual condition of mankind prior to the flood has certainly been duplicated in these end time days. *"But mark this: There will be terrible times in the last days. People will be lovers of themselves, lovers of money, boastful, proud, abusive, disobedient to parents, ungrateful, unholy, without love, unforgiving, slanderous, without self-control, brutal, not lovers of the good, treacherous, rash, conceited, lovers of pleasure rather than lovers of God - having a form of godliness but denying its power"* (2 Timothy 3:1-5).

These predictions from the 1st century AD are startlingly accurate - but the Lord was impressing on me not the CONDITIONS of those times but the CHRONOLOGY - "as it was in the DAYS of Noah", and in "the DAYS before the flood." This was revolutionary thinking to me. I was on the verge of some exciting discoveries. "From now on I will tell you of NEW things, of HIDDEN things unknown to you" (Isaiah 48:6). My first surprise was to realise that the FLOOD has more chronology tied up with it than perhaps any other event (except the cross) in the Bible.

133

Even Noah's birthday is recorded! But before invest-igating Noah's log book, for the sake of correct chronological sequence let us first consider the "DAYS before the FLOOD."

The Days before the Flood

The length of the days before the flood are distinct because of the their duration eg. Adam 930 years, Meth-uselah 969 years, Noah 950 years etc. (Genesis 5). End-less heat and argument have arisen over attempts to plot these years backwards, despite the fact that there are demonstrable gaps in these genealogies (see appendix 1). But the confusion disappears when one stops plot-ting backwards to try and find a DATE for the ANTI-QUITY of man, and plots them forwards to find the FATE OF THE INIQUITY OF MAN. Reckon on the re-vealed years and all makes sense! Remember chronophecy is for the benefit of later generations - but especially the LAST.

The Computer Feed-Off (Dia.54)

Plot these years as REDEMPTIVE years into our compu-ter and the feed-out years resulting have mind boggling qualities. So let's start with Adam who lived 930 years. Not all of these years were redemptive years as Adam initially lived in Eden in fellowship with God. I wanted to know exactly how long Adam was in the Garden of Eden. The answer does not lie on the surface. Re-member there are "hidden things" (Isaiah 48:6) in Scripture.

The Lord brought to my attention that Enoch lived for 365 years, Noah was in the Ark for 365 days exactly (see new Scofield Bible p.12 - note 4) and that a newly mar-ried couple was to spend the first 365 days of marriage without the distractions of business or war. (Deuteronomy 24:5) The seller of a house retained the right of redemption a full year after its sale (Leviticus 25:29) "Thou crownest the YEAR with Thy goodness" (Psalm 65:11). If we assume at this stage that Adam was

134

in the garden for a full year an interesting pattern emerges:-

After 365 days Adam was DRIVEN OUT of Eden.

After 365 years Enoch was LIFTED OUT of this world.

After 365 days Noah was CALLED OUT into a new world.

After 365 days the husband was SENT OUT to war or work.

After 365 days the seller was SOLD OUT to the new owner.

If we assume that Adam was driven out after one full year, and if we count the REDEMPTIVE years from AE (after Eden) an incredible chronological prophetic pattern emerges, that confirms that it was indeed 365 days that Adam enjoyed fellowship with God. So counting in AE years (after Eden) fallen Adam lived 929 years. Now remember as it was "in the DAYS before the flood, so shall it be" prior to the Lord's return. This sixth millennium that is to parallel the first millennium before the Kingdom age commences started, if you recall when we did the Times of the Millennia, in 1019 AD. (see p.34 Dia.9). Plotting fallen Adam's 929 years from 1019 AD we come to our most significant prophetic year 1948 AD!! We read "Adam, who is a type of the one who is to come" (Romans 5:14 Wuest) (Dia.54)

There is also a hexagonal geometric structure of chronophecy that brings out very clearly that 1019 AD is the key prophetic median; but that would require another book, and as the rapture is so near, I dare not delay publication any longer!

After the death of Christ the Church was born; after the death of Adam Israel was born.

Enoch in Prophecy

Enoch lived 365 years and is still living because "God took him away" (Genesis 5:24). The important factor in chronophecy is that he lived 57 years after the death of Adam (Dia.54). We have just seen how Adam points

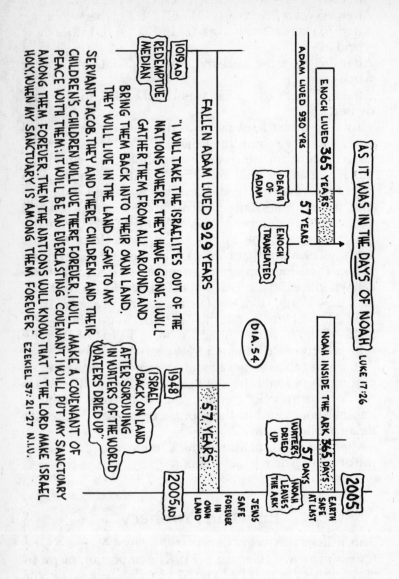

AS IT WAS IN THE DAYS OF NOAH LUKE 17:26

ADAM LIVED 930 YRS

ENOCH LIVED 365 YEARS

DEATH OF ADAM

57 YEARS

ENOCH TRANSLATED

NOAH INSIDE THE ARK 365 DAYS

2005

WATERS DRIED UP

57 DAYS

NOAH LEAVES THE ARK

EARTH SAFE AT LAST

DIA. 54

REDEMPTIVE MEDIAN

1019 AD

FALLEN ADAM LIVED 929 YEARS

1948

57 YEARS

2005 AD

ISRAEL BACK ON LAND AFTER SURVIVING IN WATERS OF THE WORLD "WATERS DRIED UP"

IN OWN LAND

JEWS SAFE FOREVER

"I WILL TAKE THE ISRAELITES OUT OF THE NATIONS WHERE THEY HAVE GONE. I WILL GATHER THEM FROM ALL AROUND, AND BRING THEM BACK INTO THEIR OWN LAND. THEY WILL LIVE IN THE LAND I GAVE TO MY SERVANT JACOB. THEY AND THERE CHILDREN AND THEIR CHILDREN'S CHILDREN WILL LIVE THERE FOREVER. I WILL MAKE A COVENANT OF PEACE WITH THEM; IT WILL BE AN EVERLASTING COVENANT. I WILL PUT MY SANCTUARY AMONG THEM FOREVER. THEN THE NATIONS WILL KNOW THAT I THE LORD MAKE ISRAEL HOLY, WHEN MY SANCTUARY IS AMONG THEM FOREVER". EZEKIEL 37: 21-27 N.I.V.

136

prophetically to 1948 AD. Now adding Enoch's additional 57 years brings us exactly to our terminal year 2005 AD. (Dia.54 & 55)

Note that 929 plus 57 = 986 years, as we saw in the Times of the Millennias. 986 solar years equal 1000 prophetic years (Dia.9 p.34). This corresponds exactly to the belief of many in the early Church that Enoch is one of the two witnesses who defy Antichrist for 3½ years and are then killed but resurrected and translated (Revelation 11:3-12). Enoch is prominently associated with second coming teaching in the New Testament. *"Enoch, the seventh from Adam, prophesied...see the Lord is coming with thousands upon thousands of His holy ones to judge everyone, and to convict all the ungodly of all the ungodly acts they have done in the ungodly way, and of all the harsh words ungodly sinners have spoken against Him."* (Jude 14-15)

For evidence that the two witnesses minister during the last 3½ years of the tribulation see 'The Revelation of Jesus Christ' (p.177 John F. Walvoord).

"The first prophecy ever given through a man (Jude 14-15), like the last (Revelation 22:20) has to do, not with Christ's first coming in grace to bring salvation, but with his second coming in judgment" (Jude by S. Maxwell Coder p.89)

Note the expression 'UNGODLY'. It simply means without. An unhappy person is one without happiness, an uneducated person is one without education. Your clean living friendly neighbour who is living his life to the full but without God is one of the UNGODLY upon whom the judgment of God must inevitably fall (2 Peter 2:4-8). *"In due time Christ died for the UNGODLY"* (Romans 5:6), but if we fail to respond to the love of God revealed on Calvary then in DUE TIME Christ will judge the UNGODLY. Today, more than ever Christians need the admonition of Spurgeon:- "I charge you who profess to be the Lord's not to be unbelieving with regard to the terrible threatenings of God to the UNGODLY. Believe the threat, even though it should

137

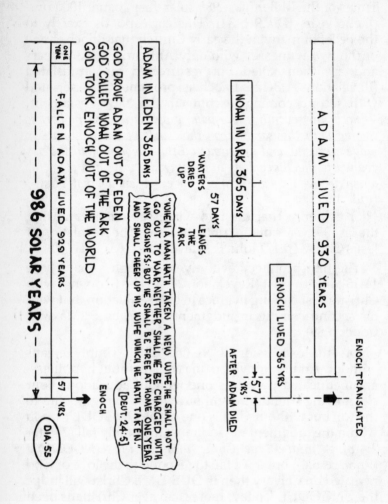

ENOCH TRANSLATED

ADAM LIVED 930 YEARS

AFTER ADAM DIED

ENOCH LIVED 365 YRS
57 YRS.

NOAH IN ARK 365 DAYS

57 DAYS

LEAVES THE ARK

"WATERS DRIED UP"

ADAM IN EDEN 365 DAYS

"WHEN A MAN HATH TAKEN A NEW WIFE, HE SHALL NOT GO OUT TO WAR, NEITHER SHALL HE BE CHARGED WITH ANY BUSINESS: BUT HE SHALL BE FREE AT HOME ONE YEAR, AND SHALL CHEER UP HIS WIFE WHICH HE HATH TAKEN."

[DEUT. 24:5]

ENOCH

GOD DROVE ADAM OUT OF EDEN
GOD CALLED NOAH OUT OF THE ARK
GOD TOOK ENOCH OUT OF THE WORLD

ONE YEAR

FALLEN ADAM LIVED 929 YEARS

57 YRS

986 SOLAR YEARS

DIA. 55

138

chill your blood; believe though nature shrinks from the overwhelming doom, for, if you do not believe, the act of disbelieving God about one point will drive you to disbelieve Him upon the other parts of revealed truth, and you will never come to that true, childlike faith which God will accept and honor.''

(Quoted in Hebrews. John MacArthur p.276)

Methuselah in Prophecy (Dia.56)

Methuselah has the distinction of living longer than any other human being on earth, he lived 969 years (Genesis 5:27). Plotting 969 years from our prophetic median 1019 AD we come to 1988 AD (the year this book was published). This year is exactly 40 years from the birth of modern Israel in 1948 - surely we will see significant developments with Israel this year, as mentioned earlier under 'Waypoint No.6' p.98.

According to the Companion Bible and the Anglican Speakers Commentary, Methuselah's name means ''At his death it shall be sent'' i.e. the DELUGE, and he actually died the year of the FLOOD - according to Jewish tradition, seven days before the FLOOD. So God extended his life span to demonstrate His long suffering (2 Peter 3:9). But God will not forever bear the consequences of man's sin - the outgrowth of man's sin was the terminating judgment of the flood. When terminal grace is up, then there is the elimination of those who persist in their evil ways.

Hence a time limit is put on their occupation of planet earth.

If we extend 969 years we have $969 \times 365.24 \div 360 = 983$ years.

Plotting 983 years on from the prophetic meridian 1019 AD we come to the year 2002 AD - the very year ''the great tribulation'' starts, when the world once more has reached terminal grace - the full extent of the longsuffering of God. Only this time it will not be WATER but FIRE that consumes the wicked. *''The whole world will be*

139

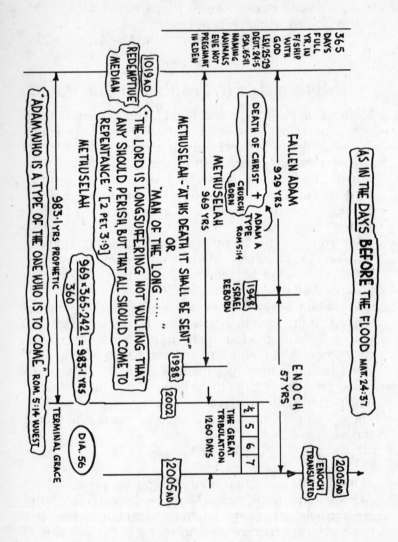

AS IN THE DAYS BEFORE THE FLOOD MAT. 24:37

365 DAYS
FULL YR. IN F'SHIP WITH GOD
LEV. 25:29
DEUT. 24:5
PSA. 65:11
NAMING ANIMALS
EVE NOT PREGNANT IN EDEN

1019 AD

REDEMPTIVE MEDIAN

DEATH OF CHRIST
CHURCH BORN
ROM 5:14
ADAM A TYPE

FALLEN ADAM
929 YRS

METHUSELAH - "AT HIS DEATH IT SHALL BE SENT"

METHUSELAH
969 YRS

1948
ISRAEL REBORN

"THE LORD IS LONGSUFFERING NOT WILLING THAT ANY SHOULD PERISH, BUT THAT ALL SHOULD COME TO REPENTANCE" [2 PET. 3:9]

"MAN OF THE LONG ....."
OR

1988

METHUSELAH

$$969 \times 365.2421 = 983.1 \text{ YRS}$$
360

983.1 YRS PROPHETIC

"ADAM, WHO IS A TYPE OF THE ONE WHO IS TO COME". ROM. 5:14 WUEST

2002

TERMINAL GRACE

DIA. 56

ENOCH
57 YRS

4 5 6 7

THE GREAT TRIBULATION
1260 DAYS

2005 AD

ENOCH TRANSLATED

2005 AD

consumed by the FIRE of my jealous anger'' (Zephaniah 3:8 NIV).

''The Lord is longsuffering, not willing that any should perish, but that all should come to repentance.'' (2 Peter 3:9).

*Note:- The waypoints can be extended or reduced by just altering the solar/prophetic ratio e.g.-

Extended $1260 \times 365.24 \div 360 = 1278$ days

Reduced $1260 \times 360 \div 365.24 = 1242$ days

CHAPTER NINE

The Days of Noah (Matthew 24:27)

"When there seemed little hope of the godly line being able to withstand the influence of the ungodly, the Flood came and left Noah's family with freedom in a new world." (The Expositor's Bible)

There is a hive of chronological activity around the flood period (Genesis 7 & 8) - nothing around the Babel period (Genesis 11). Man's great edifice of rebellion, the Tower of Babel, does not merit a day of notice on God's calendar - but the redemption of righteous Noah is detailed to the very days!

In chronophecy it is only dated bible events that are important, and should be used for projecting into end time calculations. Creation and the translation of Elijah (2 Kings 2:11) would have been interesting datum points, but they are undated, and therefore no attempt has been made to incorporate them into this scheme of chronophecy. This work has been based on careful calculations - not hazy conjectures.

If we add up the ages revealed in Genesis 5 and 9:28 deducting one year from Adam as explained earlier we have: Adam + 2005 years = 2005 AE (after Eden).

Thus the very "days of NOAH" come up with the same figures as our terminal year 2005!

There are two 365 lengths bisected with a terminal length of 57 in early Genesis both highly significant in chronophecy. Enoch lived 365 years on earth, 57 of them after Adam died. Noah was in the ark for exactly 365 days (new Scofield Bible) but 57 days before the end of his confinement *"the water had dried up from the earth"* (Genesis 8:13-14). The months were 30 day months - so the first month was 30 days plus 27 days of the second month equalling 57 days.

Noah has been consistently pictured by prophetic writers as a type of the Jewish race preserved through the waters of judgment, the waters being the Gentile nations (Revelations 17:15). In 1948 "the waters dried up" so to speak. Israel was on dry land once more in having been delivered from 80 nations, but the ground is still soggy. It's still not safe to walk on it freely. Noah had to wait another 57 days (Dia.54) before they were safe.

So Israel since 1948, has been waiting for its final security in a new world. 57 years later in 2005 AD the Jews will be secure in their land forever! *"I will take the Israelites out of the nations where they have gone. I will gather them from all around, and bring them back into their own land. They will live in the land I gave to my servant Jacob. They and their children and their children's children will live there forever.*

"I will make a covenant of peace with them; it will be an everlasting covenant. I will put my sanctuary among them forever. Then the nations will know that I the Lord make Israel holy, when my sanctuary is among them forever." (Ezekiel 37:21-28)

"Do not fear, O Jacob my servant; do not be dismayed O Israel. I will surely save you out of a distant place, your descendants from the land of their exile. Jacob will again have PEACE and SECURITY, and no one will make him afraid." (Jeremiah 46:27)

144

CHAPTER TEN

The "J" Factor (Dia.57)

So far in this study we have seen multiple bearings converging into the year 2005 AD. Let's turn our attention now to the importance of the year 1999 AD. Plotting back seven years from 2005 AD brings us to 1999 AD (Dia.64).

These seven years are years of 360 days and thus 36 days shorter than seven calendar years of 365.24 days. They are known as the 70th week of Daniel and Revelation 6-19 is a detailed account of the events of this clean up period of planet earth (see appendix two). This period will see the culmination of man's rebellion against God headed up by Antichrist; and God intervening directly in the affairs of men, flushing out, burning up and sweeping away the appalling social, moral, physical and spiritual pollution.

To this end we will consider the "J" or Judgment factor as revealed in the spiritual significance of the numbers nine and nineteen (10 + 9) in scripture.

Before calculators accountants used what they called the "K" factor - taking out the nines to check their results. We will learn the "J" factor - dividing by nine to check the biblical time spans that end in judgment.

First of all why use the number nine? Dr Bullinger in his book "Number in Scripture" says:- "Nine is the number of finality or judgment. The number nine is a most remarkable number in many respects. It is held in great reverence by all who study the occult sciences; and in mathematical science it possesses properties and powers which are found in no other number. It is the LAST of the digits, and thus marks the end; and is significant of the CONCLUSION of a matter." It is an absolute rule that whatever number you multiply by the digit nine, the sum of the digits in the product will always be nine e.g. $9 \times 3 = 27$ $2 + 7 = 9$; $7834 \times 9 = 70506$ $7 + 0 + 5 + 0 + 6 = 18$, $1 + 8 = 9$.

Now take any number say, 87594, reverse the number which gives you 49578, subtract the lesser from the greater - $87594 - 49578 = 38016$

Now add up the sum of the digits in the remainder $3 + 8 + 0 + 1 + 6 = 18$, $1 + 8 = 9$. Nine is the inescapable number of judgment. *"How shall we escape if we neglect so great salvation?"* (Hebrews 2:3)

"In Hebrew the value nine is the letter teth picturing a snake rising up in opposition against the Lamb of God." (Wonders of the Hebrew Alphabet - Steele - Smith).

When a snake rises up to attack there is no other recourse than to deal it a FINAL death dealing blow. It is incredible to find how many time spans in the Bible which end in judgment are perfectly divisible by nine. The time span from Adam to the Flood on revealed years is 1656 (184×9). When the Kingdom was divided in 930 BC the ten tribes lasted for 207 years (23×9) before being led off into captivity in 723 BC by the Assyrians (2 Kings 17). Judah's final judgment came in 70 AD - which from 930 BC is exactly 999 years! From 70 AD to 2005 AD is 1935 years (215×9). From the end of the ten tribes of Israel in 723 BC to 2005 AD is 2727 years (303×9). (See Dia.57).

Nineteen in Scripture

Bullinger just makes this brief comment "Nineteen is a number not without significance. It is a combination of $10 + 9$, and would denote the perfection of divine order connected with JUDGMENT."

The Nineteen Kings of Judah

There were exactly 19 Kings of Judah then judgment (Athalia, was an evil usurper and this woman is not counted in the line - 2 Kings 11:1-3).

146

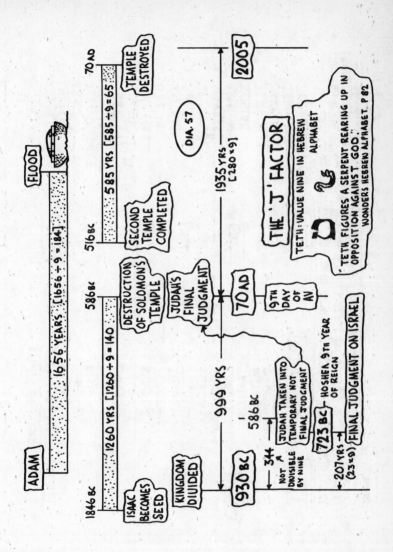

ADAM

FLOOD

1846 BC

1656 YEARS [1656 ÷ 9 = 184]

586 BC

516 BC

70 AD

TEMPLE DESTROYED

585 YRS [585 ÷ 9 = 65]

SECOND TEMPLE COMPLETED

DESTRUCTION OF SOLOMON'S TEMPLE

JUDAH'S FINAL JUDGMENT

1260 YRS [1260 ÷ 9 = 140]

ISAAC BECOMES SEED

KINGDOM DIVIDED

930 BC

999 YRS

586 BC

JUDAH TAKEN INTO TEMPORARY NOT FINAL JUDGMENT

3⁴⁴

NOT DIVISIBLE BY NINE

723 BC HOSHEA 9TH YEAR OF REIGN

207 YRS (23×9) FINAL JUDGMENT ON ISRAEL

70 AD

9TH DAY OF AV

1935 YRS [280×9]

2005

DIA. 57

THE 'J' FACTOR

TETH: VALUE NINE IN HEBREW ALPHABET

"TETH FIGURES A SERPENT REARING UP IN OPPOSITION AGAINST GOD." WONDER'S HEBREW ALPHABET. P 82

147

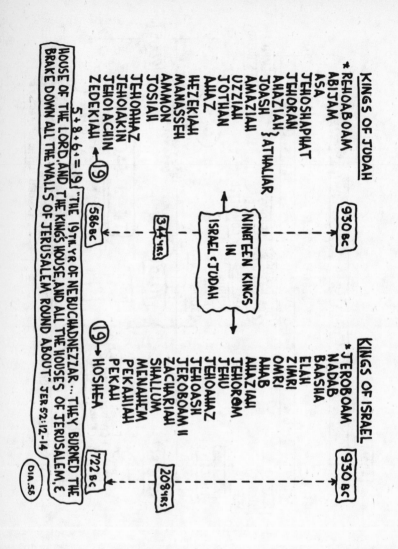

KINGS OF JUDAH

* REHOBOAM
ABIJAM
ASA
JEHOSHAPHAT
JEHORAM
AHAZIAH } ATHALIAH
JOASH
AMAZIAH
UZZIAH
JOTHAN
AHAZ
HEZEKIAH
MANASSEH
AMMON
JOSIAH
JEHOAHAZ
JEHOIAKIM
JEHOIACHIN
ZEDEKIAH → ⑲

NINETEEN KINGS
IN
ISRAEL & JUDAH

KINGS OF ISRAEL

* JEROBOAM
NADAB
BAASHA
ELAH
ZIMRI
OMRI
AHAB
AHAZIAH
JEHORAM
JEHU
JEHOAHAZ
JEHOASH
JEROBOAM II
ZACHARIAH
SHALLUM
MENAHEM
PEKAHIAH
PEKAH
⑲→ HOSHEA

930 BC   586 BC   344 YRS   930 BC   722 BC   208 YRS

5 + 8 + 6 = 19

"THE 19TH. YR OF NEBUCHADNEZZAR ... THEY BURNED THE HOUSE OF THE LORD, AND THE KINGS HOUSE, AND ALL THE HOUSES OF JERUSALEM, & BRAKE DOWN ALL THE WALLS OF JERUSALEM ROUND ABOUT." JER 52:12-14

DIA.56

148

"In the NINTH year of Zedekiah's reign (the 19th and last king of Judah) in the TENTH month....came King Nebuchadnezzar, King of Babylon against Jerusalem....in the NINTH day of the month was the city broken up....Now in the NINETEENTH year of Nebuchadnezzar, came Nebozarndan captain of the guard into Jerusalem, and burned the house of the Lord, and the King's house; and all the houses of Jerusalem....and the King of Babylon slew the sons of Zedekiah before his eyes, he slew also the princes of Judah, then he put out the eyes of Zedekiah, bound him in chains, and carried him to Babylon, and put him in prison till the day of his death." (Jeremiah 52) See Dia.59.

The Nineteen Kings of Israel

Just as there were nineteen Kings of Judah and then the FINALE - so there were exactly nineteen Kings of Israel then FINISH! Hoshea was the 19th and last King of Israel. "In the twelfth year of Ahaz King of Judah, began Hoshea to reign in Samaria over Israel NINE years, and he did that which was evil in the sight of the Lord... in the NINTH year of Hoshea, King of Israel, the King of Assyria took Samaria, and carried Israel away into Assyria... and the King of Assyria shut up Hoshea, and bound him in prison." (2 Kings 17) (See Dias.58 & 59).

The Nine Doomed Generations

In Genesis 5 we learn that Noah was the tenth generation from Adam - nine generations of offspring died in the flood. (Dia. 59)

The Judgment on Sin

The greatest judgment of all time occurred at the NINTH hour - "And at the NINTH hour Jesus cried with a loud voice 'My God, My God, why has thou forsaken me?" (Mark 15:37) See Dia.59

⑲ ZEDEKIAH

"IN THE **NINTH** YEAR OF HIS REIGN, IN THE **TENTH** MONTH, IN THE **TENTH** DAY OF THE MONTH, KING NEBUCHADREZZAR, KING OF BABYLON CAME AGAINST JERUSALEM.... IN THE **NINTH** DAY OF THE MONTH, THE CITY WAS BROKEN UP......

.... NOW IN THE **TENTH** DAY OF THE MONTH WHICH WAS THE **NINETEENTH** YEAR OF NEBUCHADREZZAR, CAME NEBUZARADAN CAPTAIN OF THE GUARD INTO JERUSALEM, AND BURNED THE HOUSE OF THE LORD, AND THE KING'S HOUSE; AND ALL THE HOUSES OF JERUSALEM, AND ALL THE HOUSES OF THE GREAT MEN, BURNED HE WITH FIRE...

..... AND THE KING OF BABYLON SLEW THE SONS OF ZEDEKIAH BEFORE HIS EYES; HE SLEW ALSO ALL THE PRINCES OF JUDAH. THEN HE PUT OUT THE EYES OF ZEDEKIAH, BOUND HIM IN CHAINS, AND CARRIED HIM TO BABYLON, AND PUT HIM IN PRISON TILL THE DAY OF HIS DEATH." [JER 52]

⑲ HOSHEA | 9+10=19 = FINALITY, JUDGMENT

"IN THE TWELFTH YEAR OF AHAZ KING OF JUDAH, BEGAN HOSHEA TO REIGN IN SAMARIA OVER ISRAEL **NINE** YEARS, AND HE DID THAT WHICH WAS EVIL IN THE SIGHT OF THE LORD ..... IN THE **NINTH** YEAR OF HOSHEA THE KING OF ISRAEL, THE KING OF ASSYRIA TOOK SAMARIA, AND CARRIED ISRAEL AWAY INTO ASSYRIA...." "AND THE KING OF ASSYRIA SHUT UP HOSHEA, AND BOUND HIM IN PRISON." (2 KINGS 17.)

① ADAM ② SETH ③ ENOS ④ CAINAN⑤ MAHALALEEL⑥ JARED ⑦ENOCH ⑧METHUSELAH
⑨ LAMECH — **NINE** GENERATIONS FROM ADAM – DOOMED TO FLOOD.
⑩ NOAH

"AND AT THE **NINTH** HOUR JESUS CRIED WITH A LOUD VOICE, MY GOD, MY GOD, WHY HAST THOU FORSAKEN ME? ..... AND GAVE UP THE GHOST." (MARK 15:37)

(DIA. 59)

The Child born out of Wedlock

"No one born out of wedlock shall enter the congregation of the Lord, even unto his TENTH generation." (Deuteronomy 23:2) Nine generations under judgment. So we see from these examples (more could be shown) that NINE and NINETEEN speak of FINALITY and JUDGMENT. Now every year this century is prefixed with the number 19 - this is the century of judgment - we are now approaching the decade of final nines 1990 through to 1999. (see Dia.60)

　　9 speaks of judgment

　　99 speaks of concentrated judgment

but 999 speaks of complete final judgment

3 is the number of completion - must give length, breadth and depth for full measure. So the triple nine gives us full measure. Jesus said to the doomed generation of His day - *"Fill up, then, the measure of the sin of your forefathers...I tell you the truth, all this will come on this generation."* (Matthew 23:32,36)

In 70 AD the judgment fell on Jerusalem - over a million lost their lives, the temple was totally destroyed and the remaining Jews were banished for twenty centuries of world wide dispersion exactly 999 years from 930 BC when the Kingdom was divided into Israel and Judah!!

Jesus warned the nation about this appalling disaster when He said - *"And so upon you will come all the righteous blood that has been shed on earth, from the blood of righteous Abel to the blood of Zechariah son of Berakiah, whom you murdered between the temple and the altar. I TELL YOU THE TRUTH, all this will come upon this generation."* (Matthew 23:35-36)

"Since the sins of a nation are cumulative, like a river in flood moving towards its highest tide, even so the sins of Israel had been moving through the centuries to a consummation in a particular generation and at a particular time...."*All these things,"* Christ said *"shall come upon this generation."*

The Greek word here must not be taken in the sense of

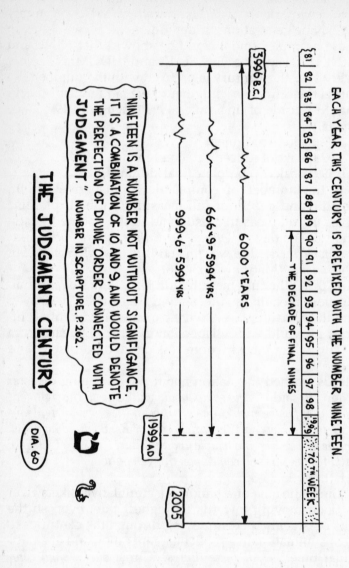

EACH YEAR THIS CENTURY IS PREFIXED WITH THE NUMBER NINETEEN.

| 81 | 82 | 83 | 84 | 85 | 86 | 87 | 88 | 89 | 90 | 91 | 92 | 93 | 94 | 95 | 96 | 97 | 98 | 99 | 70TH WEEK |

THE DECADE OF FINAL NINES

3996 B.C.

6000 YEARS

666×9 = 5994 YRS

999×6 = 5994 YRS

1999 A.D.

2005

"NINETEEN IS A NUMBER NOT WITHOUT SIGNIFICANCE. IT IS A COMBINATION OF 10 AND 9, AND WOULD DENOTE THE PERFECTION OF DIVINE ORDER CONNECTED WITH JUDGMENT." NUMBER IN SCRIPTURE. P. 262.

THE JUDGMENT CENTURY

DIA. 60

a RACE, but rather of a whole multitude of Israelites living at the time.'' (The Greatness of the Kingdom - Alva McClain p.358)

1999 AD (Dia. 60)

Just as Israel as a nation was summarily and drastically dealt with by God on the triple nine, so now God is going to square the accounts with all the nations including Israel on another triple nine-1999 AD. *''For then there will be great distress unequalled from the beginning of the world until now - and never to be equalled again... I TELL YOU THE TRUTH this generation will certainly not pass away until all these things have happened.''* (Matthew 24:21,34)

As the cumulative sins of the nation of Israel fell on one generation, so all that has characterized the age gathers into awful intensity at the end. So fearsome and horrific will be the judgments of God on a rebellious world that all heaven is hushed into an awesome momentary silence. *''When he opened the seventh seal, there was silence in heaven for about half an hour.''* (Revelation 8:1).

Have you ever noticed that twice our Lord uses the expression *''I TELL YOU THE TRUTH?''* The first was in connection with the terminal Jewish generation of His day *''I tell you the truth, all this will come upon this generation.''* (Matthew 23:36). This judgment was fulfilled to the letter in 70 AD. Secondly, Jesus connects it with our final countdown generation. *''Even so when you see all these things, you know He is near, right at the door. I tell you the truth, this generation will certainly not pass away until all these things have happened.''* (Matthew 24:33-34).

Jesus Christ tells the TRUTH - no word of His has ever failed - He warned that terminal generation of His day. The burning conflagration of the city of Jerusalem and the utter destruction of the Temple, the plagues during the siege and the taking away of the inhabitants that remained are God's object lessons to us, a smoke signal of the most ominous portent. *''I tell you the truth''* this is what will happen to all now living who fail to respond to salvation in Christ. AD 70 will be repeated again but on a world wide scale -

"They were given power over a fourth of the earth, to kill by sword, famine, and plague." (Revelation 6:8).

A third of the earth was burned up, a third of the trees were burned up, and all the green grass was burned up. (Revelation 8:7b).

A third of mankind was killed by the three plagues of fire, smoke and sulphur (Revelation 9:18).

As in AD 70, not only was the city broken up and burned (Josephus) but the people lost their freedom and were taken away as slaves. *"They will be taken as prisoners to all the nations"* (Luke 21:24), so again in the end time judgment some will be left to enter God's Kingdom, but all incorrigible rebels will be TAKEN away into judgment -

"At the coming of the Son of Man two men will be in the field, one will be taken and the other left. Two women will be grinding with a hand mill; one will be taken and the other left. Two people will be in bed, one will be taken and the other left." (Matthew 24:40-41; Luke 17:34).

N.B. These verses do not refer to the departure of the Church - the rapture is inevitably connected with resurrection (1 Thessalonians 4:14:18), but there is no reference to any resurrection in Matthew 24. (See Dia. No.4 p.20).

As the accumulated sins of the past fell on the Jewish nation in 70 AD, so again this principle will hold good during the Tribulation period. As has been well said, "Men make the guilt of past ages their own, reproduce its atrocities, identify themselves with it; and so, what seems an arbitary decree, visiting upon the children the sins of the fathers, becomes in such cases a righteous judgment." (C.J. Ellicott)

Antichrist and 1999 AD (Dia.60)

If we plot back 6000 years from 2005 AD we reach the year 3996 BC, just eight years short of Ussher's famous

The Prophecies of Nostradamus in Historical Sequence from A.D. 1550–2005

by

H.G.B. Erickstad

VANTAGE PRESS
New York / Washington / Atlanta
Los Angeles / Chicago

Doomsday 1999 A.D.

Charles Berlitz

with collaboration, maps and drawings by
J. Manson Valentine

SOUVENIR PRESS

AUGUST 1999

Frank H. Stuckert

EXPOSITION PRESS, INC.
900 South Oyster Bay Road
Hicksville, New York 11801

date of 4004 BC! If we plot antichrist's number 666 from 3996 BC (the solar terminal for our six days of redemptive chronology) by the number of judgment, 9, we have

666 x 9 = 5994 years

3996 BC + 5994 years = 1999 AD!

If we multiply triple nine, 999 (complete judgment) by 6 (the number of man) again we have 999 x 6 = 5994 years

Chronophecy certainly points to 1999 AD as the beginning of the final judgment period.

The Occult and 1999 AD (Dia.64)

We read in Revelation 12:12 the devil KNOWS his TIME is short. I hold no brief for the occult but it is surprising how frequently occult books refer to the nearness of the end of the age.

Imagine my surprise after doing all my biblical homework on the years up to 2005 AD to see in a bookseller's window a book entitled "The Prophecies of Nostradamus in Historical Sequence from AD 1500 - 2005" (H.G.B. Erickstad) (Dia. 61).

Quatrain x:72 reads "In the year 1999 and seventh month, from the skies will appear a great King of terror...he will reign for a good hour."

Another book entitled "August 1999" by Frank H. Stuckert, states, "On August 11th 1999 Sun - Saturn - Uranus - Mars will form a cross, a very rare sign in the universe." He also talks about a Bavarian prophet Alois Irlmaier who clearly sees three nines and he says, "There can be no doubt that 1999 AD is meant." (Dia. 63).

The medium Jeanne Dixon has said - Antichrist will grow mightily until 1999 at which time he will form his new religion. Charles Berlitz published a book in 1981 entitled "Doomsday 1999 AD." (Dia. 62).

Another book entitled "Armageddon - Doomsday in our Lifetime?" by Bob Leaman discussing the predictions of the great pyramid says, "There appears to be an indication in these upper passage ways of a totally new spiritual order beginning in 1999.... In the lower

158

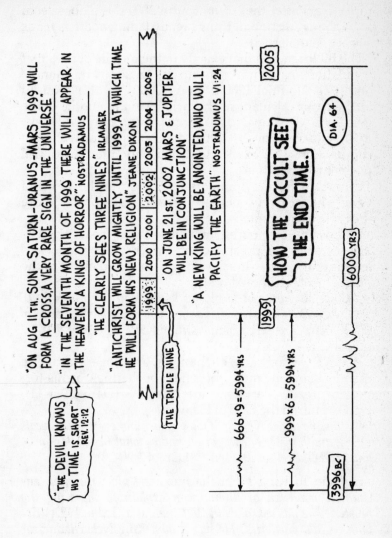

chambers an indication of the possible collapse of civilis-
ation in about 2004... It looks as if something pretty
horrific is in the offing for about 2004 - maybe two or
three years after that. But around 2004 there does seem
to be the prediction of things really falling apart as far as
society is concerned."

The Bible teaches that exactly in the middle of the great
tribulation, Antichrist sets up an image in the temple
and then the final 1260 days of God's wrath is poured
out. On our calculations that will be in the middle of the
year 2002 AD. Now Nostradamus in quatrain V1:24 says
in effect "On June 21st 2002 Mars and Jupiter will be in
conjunction. A new King will be anointed who will
pacify the earth."

Christians have a complete revelation in the Word of
God. The heavenly bodies served as signposts before
the Bible was completed.

When one compares European and Eastern predictions with the precise clear cut chronological predictions of the Bible, it's like comparing candlelight to the
brilliance of the noon day sun.

*"Come, O house of Jacob, let us walk in the LIGHT OF
THE LORD. You have abandoned your people the house of
Jacob. They are full of superstitions FROM THE EAST.'*
(Isaiah 2:6)

When the magicians, enchanters, astrologers and wise
men of Babylon could not tell Nebuchadnezzar his forgotten dream - let alone interpret it - (Daniel 2:1-11),
Daniel praised the God of Heaven.

*"Praise be to the Name of God for ever and ever...He reveals
DEEP and HIDDEN things; He knows what lies in darkness,
and LIGHT dwells with Him."* (Daniel 2:20-22).

He said to King Nebuchadnezzar *"No wise man, en-
chanter, magician or diviner can explain to the King the
mysteries he has asked about, but there is a God in HEAVEN
who reveals mysteries. He has shown King Nebuchadnezzar
what will happen in days to come."* (Daniel 2:27-28).

Be warned, reader, against every form of divination,
no matter how harmless it may appear. *"Let no one be*

found among you who practices divination or sorcery, interprets omens, engages in witchcraft, or casts spells, or who is a medium or spiritist or who consults the dead. Anyone who does these things is detestable to the Lord.'' (Deuteronomy 18:10-12). *''I am the Lord....who foils the signs of false prophets and makes fools of diviners....who carries out the words of his servants and fulfils the predictions of His messengers.''* (Isaiah 44:24-26 also Isaiah 47:9, 12-14).

1999 and Sodom and Gomorrah (Genesis 19)

Sodom was destroyed when Abraham was 99 years of age. (Two nines = concentrated judgement - Gen. 18; 10; 21:5). Abraham was born in 1951 BC., so he was 99 in the year 1852 BC. We learnt that from the weaning of Isaac 1846 BC. adding 3850 years (1260 + 2520 + 70) came to 2005 AD. (p.100), and converting to prophetic to 1949 - both good years for Israel. Note 3850 = 77 x 50 (Jubilee Lev 25:11-15). Forgiveness extends its limit to ''Seventy seven times'' (Mat. 18:21 NIV).

If we add 3850 years to the year God rained fire and brimstone on Sodom and Gomorrah 1852 BC., it comes to the triple nine 1999 AD. - the start of the Tribulation and the outpouring of the wrath of God on a Christ rejecting world (Rev.6-18). If we convert to prophetic years it comes to 1943 AD; the year the U.S. Air Force joined Bomber Command in the saturation bombing of the nation that was systematically annihilating the Jews - NAZI GERMANY. On the night of August 23rd, 1943 I personally flew on a bombing raid over Berlin when more bombs in tonnage were dropped in this single 'operation' than were dropped on England in the whole war!

Surely 1999 AD. will see the judgment on Sodom and Gomorrah duplicated on a world wide scale. *''As it was in the DAYS OF LOT, so shall it be also in the DAYS OF THE SON OF MAN.''* (Luke 17:26-28 KJV). Sodom means 'fettered' and Gomorrah means 'bondage'. The world out of Christ are the SLAVES OF SATAN *"the whole world is under the control of the evil one"* (1 John 5:19 NIV). God will start releasing those fetters in 1999 and the third Exodus for ISRAEL and believing Gentiles will be accomplished in 2005 AD!

Remember Lot was delivered BEFORE God destroyed Sodom (Gen. 19:22-23); a picture of the church raptured BEFORE the Tribulation. (see p.173-175), but be warned! Lot's deliverance did not include family salvation. (*"Remember Lot's wife"* Luke 17:32, Ezek. 14:12-21).

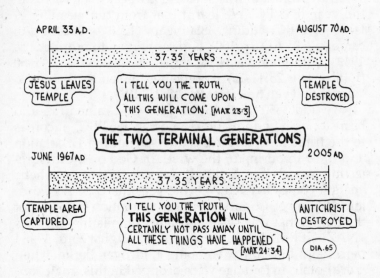

APRIL 33 A.D.   AUGUST 70 AD.

37·35 YEARS

JESUS LEAVES TEMPLE

"I TELL YOU THE TRUTH, ALL THIS WILL COME UPON THIS GENERATION." [MAT. 23:3]

TEMPLE DESTROYED

THE TWO TERMINAL GENERATIONS

JUNE 1967 AD   2005 AD

37·35 YEARS

TEMPLE AREA CAPTURED

"I TELL YOU THE TRUTH, **THIS GENERATION** WILL CERTAINLY NOT PASS AWAY UNTIL ALL THESE THINGS HAVE HAPPENED" [MAT. 24:34]

ANTICHRIST DESTROYED

DIA. 65

CHAPTER ELEVEN

Chronophecy and the Two Terminal Generations (Dia.65)

The last time Jesus was in the temple, according to Hoehner, was the 1st April 33 AD. That is when He said, *"I tell you the truth, all this will come upon this generation."* (Matthew 23:3). In early August 70 AD the temple and Jerusalem were destroyed by the Romans, giving us a time span of 37.35 years.

When Israeli paratroopers recaptured Old Jerusalem and the temple area in June 1967 AD, one of their historians wrote:- "We are at the stage where David was when he liberated Jerusalem. From that time until the construction of the temple by Solomon, only ONE GENERATION passes, so will it be with us." (Israel Eldad).

"In the year 996 BC a man of Judah, King David, successfully breached Jerusalem's defences, and fixed its destiny for all time as the epicentre of the mono-thiestic world" ('Dome of the Rock' Landay p.27). In 959 BC Solomon's temple was finished (1 Kings 6:38), an exact period of 37 years!"

If God repeats the same time span as He did for the first generation, then plotting from early June 1967 AD 37.35 years we come to 2004.8 AD! Remember how many times 1967 came up during this study.

Will this be the time that Malachi refers to? *"Then suddenly the Lord you are seeking will come to His temple....so I will come near to you for judgment. I will be quick to testify against sorcerers, adulterers and perjurers, against those who defraud labourers of their wages, who oppress the widows and the fatherless, and deprive aliens of justice, but do not FEAR ME. says the Lord Almighty."* (Malachi 3:1,5 NIV).

163

In the light of all the previous positive scriptural and historic evidence pointing to 2005 AD it would appear to be all but a dead certainty. Surely, surely *"He is near, even at the door. I tell you the truth this generation will certainly not pass away until all these things have happened."* (Matthew 24:34).

The likelihood of this second span of 37.35 years occurring is made more feasible when we consider that this is exactly how God has operated in the past! We see this cyclic pattern in history - remember the exact repetition of those four time spans in the perfect symmetry of the TIMES OF THE TEMPLES? Do you remember those 1915 years (Dia.48) from Isaac to 70 AD repeated in the 1915 years from Pentecost 33 AD through to Israel's birth in 1948 AD? We see the same repeated pattern in scripture e.g. *"After 70 years are accomplished at Jerusalem I will visit you"* (Jeremiah 29:10), *"Tyre shall be forgotten 70 years."* (Isaiah 23:15).

In the Companion Bible appendix 50:V11 there are five time spans of 490 years in scriptural chronology. Further examples of specific recurring periods of time are given in the Anglican "Speaker's Commentary" on Isaiah (introduction p.7) and Sir Robert Anderson's "The Coming Prince" (Appendix 1).

How much more evidence does God have to give you before you realise that it's practically all over bar the shouting?

Our Lord rebuked the religious leaders of His day on this very issue *"O ye hypocrites, ye can discern the face of the sky; but can ye not discern the SIGNS OF THE TIME?"* (Matthew 16:3).

They knew more about meterology than they did about eschatology! (The study of the Last Times). As J.J. Van Oosterzee has well said - "It lies in the nature of the case that christian eschatology, the more the course of time advances, must become less and less an unimportant appendix, and more and more a locus primarius of Christian doctrine." (Lange's commentary on Luke p.326).

That terminal generation of 70 AD suffered according

to our Lord's commentary on the situation. *"They will dash you to the ground, you and the children within your walls. They will not leave one stone on another, BECAUSE you did not recognise the TIME of God's coming to you."* (Luke 19:44).

Dr. Roy Hicks says :- "It is only right and proper for the Holy Spirit to emphasise this great truth (the rapture) now, because of the imminence of events leading up to a catastrophic climax." (Another look at the Rapture p.118). Paul informs Christians - *"but you brethren are not in darkness so that the day of the Lord should surprise you like a thief."* (1 Thessalonians 5:4).

All systems are GO. He could be raising His trumpet right now! Do you recognise THE TIME of God's coming for YOU? The great tragedy will be that main stream society will be in complete ignorance till the flood waters of God's judgment hits them! *"For in the days before the flood, people were eating and drinking, marrying and giving in marriage, up to the day Noah entered the ark; AND THEY KNEW NOTHING ABOUT WHAT WOULD HAPPEN until the flood came and took them all away. That is how it will be at the coming of the Son of Man."* (Matthew 24:38-39).

Peter tells us that in these last days scoffers are *"willingly ignorant"* (2 Peter 3:5KJV). They just do not want to know! Not looking for Christ's return. Expecting the sun to keep ever shining on their plans - the thought of global catastrophic disaster is abhorrent to them.

Learn from Sodom - *"By the time Lot reached Zoar, the SUN had risen over the land* (O what a lovely, pleasant day!) *Then the Lord rained down burning sulphur on Sodom and Gomorrah - from the Lord out of the heavens. Thus he overthrew those cities and the entire plain, including all those living in the cities - and also the vegetation in the land."* (Genesis 19:23-26).

Mount St. Helens March 1980

"It had been building up for weeks. The rumbling began on March 25th. Mount St. Helens in south western Washington continued sending out warning signals with increasing intensity and frequency through all of April and more than half of May.

Geologists indicated that, after more than 175 years of inactivity, the volcanic peak was unquestionably going to erupt. State officials warned people to remain well away from the mountain and attempted to move local residents out of the area.

One local businessman, crusty 84 year old Harry A. Truman (no relative to the former U.S. president) refused to budge from his lodge on Spirit Lake - part way up Mount St. Helens. He became something of a celebrity, declaring that he and his sixteen cats would survive any eruption by holing up in a nearby mine shaft "with a couple of bottles of whisky." Harry maintained that since Spirit Lake was his home he would "spit in the eye" of the mountain, remaining there "till hell freezes over."

Numerous others - newsmen, campers, mountain climbers and outdoor lovers - ignored warnings and continued to move about, on, or near the restive volcano.

Then suddenly, at 8.35 a.m. on Sunday May 18th, Mount St. Helens erupted in the space of seconds with a blast that could be felt and heard over 200 miles away! The force of that eruption shot a column of rock and ash nine miles into the air and scattered volcanic ash and dust over six states and three provinces - in some locales to a depth of several feet - darkening the sky in a wide area of Washington State, creating floods, and sending boiling mud down the ruptured mountainside. The blast was said to be equal to the most powerful nuclear explosion ever set off by man.

Over 70 persons, including Harry Truman and his cats, perished - many of them succumbing to the intense heat and / or gases emitted in the eruption. The majority of the bodies could not be located and the missing persons were officially declared dead by state decree after two weeks of intensive search.

Dead - because they disregarded the warning and

underestimated the danger! (Apocalypse Next - William Goetz).

Harry Truman had fifty-five days of warning - how many is God going to give you?

Flight TE 901 to Mount Erebus

On November 28th, 1979, New Zealand's largest air disaster occurred. At 8.17 a.m. an Air New Zealand D.C. 10 ZK.NZP took off from Auckland for a scenic flight to Antarctica with 257 people on board. The 257 passengers were enjoying to the full the comfort of their cabins, the light-hearted conversation, the clicking of numerous cameras, and at midday were busy enjoying an excellent lunch, utterly oblivious of impending catastrophe. They had descended to 1500 ft. when with only six seconds warning they flew through a whiteout into the mass of the 12,450 ft high Mount Erebus.

Four hours thirty one minutes after leaving Auckland they were ushered permanently into eternity. White out - then WIPE OUT!

Tasman Bridge - Hobart Tasmania

In 1974, with my wife Coral and 9 year old son Dennis, I was busy conducting crusades throughout the beautiful island of Tasmania. Spanning the Derwent River at Hobart was the imposing high arched Tasman Bridge. In the darkness of Christmas Eve 1975, a ship collided with the bridge's tall support columns, collapsing a large section of the bridge. Cars driving up the high arch could not see that half the bridge was missing and plunged helplessly into the Derwent many feet below. Frantic, desperate signals were made to stop them, but a number raced past every warning light hurtling their passengers into eternity.

SCORN THE WARNING AND YOU WILL NEVER SEE THE MORNING!

586 BC The Fall of Jerusalem

"The Lord, the God of their fathers, sent word to them through His messengers AGAIN and AGAIN, because He had pity on His people and on HIS dwelling place. But they mocked God's messengers, despised His words, and scoffed at HIS prophets until the wrath of God was aroused against His people and there was NO REMEDY." (2 Chronicles 36:15-16)

70 AD The Fall of Jerusalem

"O Jerusalem, Jerusalem, you who kill the prophets and stone those who are sent unto you, how often I have longed to gather your children together, as a hen gathers her chicks under her wings, but you were not willing. Look your house is left to you desolate." (Matthew 23:37-38 KJV).

CHAPTER TWELVE

World War 1 in Chronophecy (Dia.66)

Do you remember in the Times of the Gentiles 2590 years added to 586 BC yielded 2005 AD, and converting to prophetic years it came to 1967 AD? (p.41). Also we saw the same phenomenon in the Times of the Temples - 2628 years added to 624 BC came to 2005 AD. Converting to prophetic years, it too came to 1967 AD. The first bearing, the Times of the Millennia plotted from 33 AD also came to 2005 AD. If we plot back 6000 solar years (the full bearing) we come to 3996 BC the terminus a quo of redemptive chronology. Now converting 6000 solar years into prophetic years 6000 x 360 ÷ 365.24 = 5913.9 years; added to 3996 BC i.e. 5913.9 - 3996 + 1 = 1918.9 AD. November 1918! The eleventh of November 1918 was ARMISTICE DAY - what bearing does this day have on the Jewish nation?

Remember 12 months earlier the Balfour Declaration was issued and England had committed herself to a policy advocating the return of the Jews to Palestine. ''Balfour, Lloyd George, Churchill, General Smuts and some others were Bible lovers and Bible believers who had been brought up to believe in the return of the Jews to Palestine as a Messianic move of God. It is to their eternal credit that when the time came they rose to their responsibilities and let God use them, because they had faith in the word of God. The Balfour Declaration was the hinge upon which the Jewish - Zionist gate swung open. After 1900 years of exile, tribulation and suffering the way was open - the way home.'' (The Fall & Rise of Israel p.124-125 Hull).

After General Allenby had conquered Jerusalem, his army continued northwards driving the Turks out of

3996 B.C.

6000 SOLAR YEARS

2005 A.D.

6000 × 360 ÷ 365·24 = 5913·9 YEARS

WORLD WAR ONE ENDED AT ELEVEN A.M.
ON NOVEMBER 11, 1918, WHICH WAS:

THE ELEVENTH HOUR
OF THE ELEVENTH DAY
JUST ELEVEN DAYS AFTER THE SURRENDER OF THE TURKS,
OF THE ELEVEN MONTH OF THE YEAR 1918,
JUST ELEVEN MONTHS AFTER ALLENBY ENTERED JERUSALEM
ON THE ELEVENTH DAY OF DECEMBER, 1917.

1918·9 A.D.
= NOV. 1918
ARMISTICE

WORLD WAR ONE IN CHRONOPHECY

DIA 66

Palestine and finally an armistice was signed on October 31st 1918. The fact that Turkey stopped fighting immediately after the Euphrates River was reached seemed to indicate an amazing act of God. Abraham had been promised the land between the River of Egypt and the Euphrates River (Genesis 15:18). For many centuries this land had been in the hands of the Moslems; Israel was in exile. But now the time had come for Israel to return. The nest was being stirred, hearts were moved to return, and the land must be emptied of Islam to make possible the reoccupation by Israel.

Nothing but a war could persuade the Turks to give up that territory, so God permitted a world-wide war to break out. Palestine was the keystone to be set in place. Lord Balfour later expressed the conviction that the founding of the Jewish National Home was the most significant outcome of the First World War. It might be hard to accept the thought that such a conflagration would have been permitted by God for such a tiny bit of land. But it was not the tiny bit of land that mattered; the important thing was that God should keep His word - His promise to Israel to bring them back again to their own land. Let us consider how significant it was that immediately the land had been cleared from one boundary to the other, the slaughter and destruction was caused to cease. The war had been raging for four years, but within ELEVEN DAYS after the Holy Land had been cleared it came to an abrupt stop all over the world on November 11th 1918. God's purpose was fulfilled.

"Nations are in uproar, Kingdoms fall,....He makes WARS CEASE.....Be still, and know that I am God; I will be exalted among the nations, I will be exalted in the earth." (Psalm 4:6,9-10).

Two world wars have had only one tangible result - the Holy Land becoming what Ezekiel called the CENTRE of the nations (Ezekiel 5:5; 38:12). For the importance of the two world wars in prophecy I recommend Lance Lambert's book 'Till the Day Dawns' under the chapter heading 'The Great Shaking' (Kingsway Publications).

CHAPTER THIRTEEN

The Great Deliverance known as the Rapture

"For the Lord Himself will come down from Heaven, with a loud command, with the voice of the archangel, and with the trumpet call of God, and the dead in Christ will rise first. After that, we who are still alive and are left, will be caught up with them in the air, and so will be with the Lord forever." (1 Thessalonians 4:16-17). The expression 'caught up' (Greek HAR-PA'-ZO) means "to seize, snatch - conveys the idea of force suddenly exercised - a forceful seizure". "W.E. Vine - Expositors Dictionary of N.T. words).

Translated else where as follows:-

"When they came out of the water, the Spirit of the Lord SUDDENLY TOOK Philip away." (Acts 8:39).

"The violent TAKE IT BY FORCE." (Matthew 11:12).

"Be merciful to those who doubt; SNATCH others from the fire and save them." (Jude 23).

The Entebbe Hostages

On the 3rd July 1976, 106 Jewish hostages were held captive in a disused terminal building at Entebbe Airport, Uganda, in fear of their lives. Their position seemed hopeless. They were well guarded; it was dark and depressing, with a rainstorm lashing the airport. At the eleventh hour, 2301 hours to be exact, 200 specially selected Israeli paratroopers touched down on a dramatic rescue mission. Just before midnight the released hostages were flown home in a Hercules aircraft. In scriptural language they were CAUGHT UP,

173

SNATCHED, FORCEFULLY TAKEN to their true home.

After the hostages were caught up, airlifted to safety (type of RAPTURE) Idi Amin (type of Antichrist) frustrated and angered at their dramatic rescue, launched an intensified reign of terror. There were mass arrests, torture and murder during his bitter reign, 300,000 people disappeared. The Christian tribes of Lango and Archoli were singled out for bitter persecution. Idi Amin assumed the titles 'Emperor' and 'Son of God'. The Anglican Archbishop of Uganda and two Christian ministers were murdered.

But three years later in 1979 his regime was toppled by Tanzania. Likewise Antichrist's 3.5 years of horror will be terminated by the glorious true Son of God. (Revelation 19:19-23) ENTEBBE THEN AMIN!

DELIVERANCE THEN DESTRUCTION

God's consistent pattern throughout the Bible is DELIVERANCE for the WHOSOEVER WILLS (Revelation 22:17), then DESTRUCTION for the WHOSOEVER WON'TS (Matthew 23:37)

"Noah entered the ark as God commanded. And AFTER the seven days the flood waters came on the earth." (Genesis 7:9-10) *"Every living thing on the face of the earth was wiped out,"* (Genesis 7:23)

"But haste thee, escape hither; for I CANNOT DO ANYTHING TILL thou be come hither..." Lot entered Zoar, THEN the Lord rained upon Sodom and Gomorrah brimstone and fire from the Lord out of Heaven. (Genesis 19:22-25).

"...the Israelites went through the sea on dry ground... The water flowed back and covered the chariots and horsemen - the entire army of Pharaoh that had FOLLOWED the Israelites into the sea. Not one of them survived." (Exodus 14:22,28)

They *"brought out Rahab, her father, and mother and brothers and all who belonged to her. They brought out her*

174

*entire family and put them in a place outside the camp of
Israel. THEN they burned the whole city and everything in
it.''* (Joshua 6:23-24)
*''When you see Jersualem surrounded by armies, you will
know that its desolation is near. THEN let those in Judea flee
to the mountains, let those in the city get out... For this is the
time of punishment in fulfilment of all that has been written.''*
(Luke 21:20-22)

In AD. 70 the ''whosever wills'' (Christians) escaped to
Pella, before the 1,000,000 ''whosoever wont's''
perished in the Roman siege and destruction of
Jerusalem.

In the light of all the multiple bearings of chronophecy
we have studied, it is the earnest conviction of the writer
that the Church will be airlifted before 1999 AD.
Probably well before, so that the harvest of evil can fully
ripen for the judgment of God. The Church is the salt of
the earth, the light of the world, and with the restraint
of the Holy Spirit removed (2 Thessalonians 2:5-8), total
corruption and gross darkness will cover the earth.

So my friend you have a choice - you can be
ENTEBBEISED (lifted) or AMINISED (sifted) through
the tribulation period of 1999-2005.

It's either the FEAST (Revelation 19:9) or the BEAST
(Revelation 13). The rapture of the church will seal the
doom of thousands who have heard the gospel but
failed to respond. The E.T.A. (estimated time of arrival)
is almost here. We can know its NEARNESS *''when you
see all these things, you know HE is NEAR''* (Matthew
24:33), but never know its EXACTNESS. *''No one knows
about the day or the hour''* (Matthew 24:36,42,44,50,
25:13).

Lets think of E.T.A. like this:-

Let E stand for ENTEBBE (RAPTURE) and A for AMIN
(THE TRIBULATION TERROR).

What is between them and what divides them is T, the
Cross of Jesus Christ, where His blood was shed. *''So
Christ was sacrificed once to take away the sins of many
people; and he will appear the second time, not to bear sin, but*

to bring salvation.'' (Hebrews 9:28)

"Since we have now been justified by HIS BLOOD, how much more shall we be saved from God's wrath through him!" (Romans 5:9)

Christians are exhorted *"to wait for His son from heaven, whom He raised from the dead - Jesus, who rescues us from the coming wrath."* (1 Thessalonians 1:10)

"For God did not appoint us to suffer wrath but to receive salvation through our Lord Jesus Christ." (1 Thessalonians 5:11)

As Dr. Roy Hicks has well said - "Some say the Church isn't ready to stand before God so it needs to be purged by the tribulation. Dearly beloved, don't buy this nonsense. If the blood of Jesus Christ, God's Son does not qualify you for Heaven, then having your head cut off, dying of starvation, or suffering in prison will not qualify you either." (Another Look at the Rapture p.53)

The first atom bomb exploded in 1945 in the New Mexico desert. The nearest town was Los Alamos (Souls in Spanish). Between them and the apocalyptic atomic death was a mountain range known as the Sangre De Christo Range, which in Spanish means 'the blood of Christ.' Your only shelter from the impending judgments and outpoured wrath of God is behind the blood of Christ.

The Israelites on their final night in Egypt were saved from God's devastating judgment because they painted the sides and the top of the door frame with the freshly slain blood of a lamb. *"The blood will be a sign for you on the houses where you are; and when I see the blood, I will pass over you."* (Exodus 12:13). Rahab lived in a house on the wall of the doomed city of Jericho. Behind her the situation was a foregone disaster - in front of her were the advancing victorious Israelites. But we read *"she tied the SCARLET CORD in the window."* (Joshua 2:21). That scarlet cord speaks of salvation through death. The cord itself would have been made from a living plant that had been cut down. *"He shall grow up before Him as a tender plant... He was CUT OFF out of the land of the living, for the transgression of my people was he stricken."*(Isaiah 53:2,8)

176

The scarlet dye used to colour the cord came from the DEATH of the kermes insect, which was crushed to extract the dye. *"He was crushed for our iniquities; the punishment that brought us peace was upon him."* (Isaiah 53)

So between "Rahab the prostitute" (Joshua 2:1,6:17,22,25) and certain death (Joshua 6:21) from the advancing Israelites, there hung A SCARLET CORD, a picture of the death of Jesus Christ who hung upon a tree, and shed his blood for our salvation.

"Without the shedding of BLOOD there is NO forgiveness". (Hebrews 9:22b). Rahab said to the Israelites *"I know that the Lord has given this land to you"* (Joshua 2:9). Throughout this book we have seen 1948 and 1967 repeatedly stressed in the chronophecy of the Bible. The fig tree (Israel) has begun to bud. *"Know that he is NEAR at the very doors* (Matthew 24:33). From May 14 1948 God began to give the land of Palestine back to the Jews. Can you say with Rahab *"I know that the Lord has given this land (Palestine) to you and that a great fear of you has fallen on us, so that all who live in this country are melting in fear because of you."* (Joshua 2:9).

Why were Rahab and her relatives saved when every other citizen of Jericho was killed?

A. Her knowledge of what God was going to do through Israel instilled in her a healthy fear of the Lord.

"That all the people of the earth might know the hand of the Lord, that it is mighty: that ye might FEAR the Lord your God for ever". (Joshua 4:24)

"The FEAR of the Lord is the BEGINNING of knowledge; but fools despise wisdom and instruction". (Proverbs 1:7)

To listen to many a preacher today one would think God is coming again with chocolate fudge and sugar candy, instead of a "rod of iron" and a "sharp sword". (Revelation 19:15;2 Thessalonians 1:7-9)

B. She obeyed implicitly the instruction the Israelites gave her. Another woman of loose morals was given the same advice by none other than Jesus Christ *"salvation is from the JEWS"* (John 4:22). Eastern religions, Western cults, tarot cards, spiritism, horoscopes, or pendulum swinging is NOT OF THE JEWS. Rahab turned her back on her pagan priests and philosophers, and acted only on JEWISH advice. Unless you bow to the Jewish born Saviour who shed His BLOOD you will be as doomed as the inhabitants of Jericho. *"Neither is there salvation in any other: for there is none other name under Heaven given among man whereby we must be saved."* (Acts 4;12).

Do not be like Naaman in your attitude. This army commander was a leper, and Elisha the prophet gave him the cure. *"Go wash yourself seven times in Jordan, and your flesh will be restored and you will be cleansed."* But *Naaman went away angry and said, "I thought that he would surely come out to me and stand and call on the name of the Lord his God, wave his hand over the spot and cure of my leprosy. Are not Abana and Pharpar, the rivers of Damascus better than any of the waters of Israel? Couldn't I wash in them and be cleansed?" So he turned and went off in rage."* (2 Kings 5:10-12). Fortunately, Naaman had a change of heart, obeyed God's directions - and was healed.

C. Rahab, the scarlet woman, tied the SCARLET CORD in the window. In other words she made her faith, her trust in the SCARLET CORD public. When the Israelites were delivered out of Egypt, they went PUBLIC about their faith in the blood of the slain lamb. The instructions for your salvation are explicit, BELIEVE, ACT and OBEY these INSTRUCTIONS NOW.

"If you CONFESS with your MOUTH (i.e. go public) 'Jesus is Lord' and BELIEVE in your heart that God raised him from the dead you will be SAVED. For it is with your heart that you believe and are justified, and it is with your mouth that you confess and are SAVED" (Romans 10:9-10). Jesus said:- *"Whoever acknowledges me before men, I will also acknowledge him before my Father in heaven. But whoever disowns me before men, I will disown him before my Father in heaven."* (Matthew 10:32-33).

Dear reader if you would like to become a Christian right now, kneel down and repeat this prayer from your heart:-

Dear Lord Jesus, realizing I am a sinner in the sight of a Holy God, and that you had to come to shed your blood for my sin - so that I could be cleansed, forgiven and given right standing before God, I receive you now as my Saviour - I am trusting entirely on what you have done at Calvary. Thank you Lord Jesus for dying for me, help me now to live for you, and to openly acknowledge you before men - for Jesus' sake. Amen.

Tell someone what you have done - get in touch with an earnest Christian for nurture and guidance in your new found faith. Join the fellowship of a church that does not tamper around with the divine inspiration of the Scriptures, is actively concerned for the lost, and supports a missionary programme.

Especially for Pastors

Dr. Andrew Bonar told a story of a plain man in one of the Scottish Presbyterian country kirks who had learned the precious doctrine of the personal return of our Lord. The man had spent some time in Edinburgh, and when he returned to his village, the people asked him how he liked the Edinburgh preachers. His reply was "they all fly on one wing. They all preach the first coming of Christ, but they do not preach His second coming." Nothing recovers evangelical fervor and rekindles missionary passion, like a realisation of the great fact that He may come at any moment.

Three fifths of the Bible is prophecy; and nine tenths, if not all, of the prophetic word converges upon the end of the age. The New Testament has over 300 references to the Second Coming one verse in every 25! As Erwin Jenkins points out:- "The best proof for the inspiration of the scripture is prophecy. But because the professing church has allowed false teachers to come in, prophecy has been neglected and laid aside as untenable. When this is done the people fall prey to every wind of doctrine, eventually disbelieving that the Bible is the word of God. Prophecy is the most sturdy rung in the ladder of the Christian faith."

The viewpoint that there are different interpretations of prophecy is a lame excuse for not developing and preaching one's own convictions. There are many views on the atonement - does that stop you preaching the cross? Dear Lord, please let me hear again preachers with urgency, conviction, authority and passion in their messages. President Valery Giscard d'Estaing of France observed:

"The present world crisis..... is not just a passing perturbation, but in reality represents a permanent change. If we examine the major graphic curves that are drawn for the future by the phenomena of our times, you see that all of these curves lead to catastrophe." (Quoted in Prophecy Fact or Fiction p.3 Josh McDowell).

Charles E. Lindblom, political scientist, says in his book "Politics and World Markets":- "Relentlessly accumulating evidence shows that human life on the planet is headed for catastrophe."

Mr. Preacher, you are sitting on a time bomb, the fuse is all but burnt out - it's not time for non-threatening, gentle, milk and water innocuous inanities. *"Son of man, I have made you a watchman for the house of Israel; so hear the word I speak and give them WARNING from me.*

When I say to the wicked, 'O wicked man, you will surely die,' and you do not speak out to dissuade him from his ways, that wicked man will die for his sin, and I will hold you accountable for his blood." (Ezekiel 33:7-8).

"Remember that for three years I never stopped WARNING each of you night and day with tears." (Acts 20:31).

"Knowing therefore the terror of the Lord, we persuade men." (2 Corinthians 5:11).

God does speak to men - now one way, now another terrifying them with warnings, to turn man from wrongdoing..... to preserve his soul from the pit, his life from perishing by the sword." (Job 33:14-18).

To Elders and Deacons

Is it the time to be temple and palace building - tying up

vast sums of money, crippling missionary programmes?

Solomon spent seven years building the temple. It took him thirteen years, however to complete the construction of his palace. (1 Kings 6:38-7:1) *"Is it a time for yourselves in your panelled houses, while this house remains a ruin?* (Haggai 1:3)

To my fellow Christians

As Paul says - *"What I mean, brothers, is that the time is short. From now on those who have wives should live as if they had none, those who mourn, as if they did not; those who are happy, as if they were not; those who buy something, as if it were not theirs to keep; those who use the things of the world, as if not engrossed in them. For this world in its present form is passing away."* (1 Corinthians 7:29-31).

My big chief during World War II was Sir Arthur Harris, Commander-in Chief of Bomber Command. He never sent a warning note days before he inspected a squadron - we never knew the DAY nor the HOUR when he would come. He would just drop in suddenly from the sky; and all hell would be let loose if the Wing Commander has been negligent in carrying out his duties!

We have been commisioned to "Preach the Gospel", not to put the world right - the ship of civilization is wrecked beyond repair.

Our task is to rescue as many as possible from the wreck before it finally founders. *"Follow me and I will make you fishers of MEN."* (Luke 5:10).

How would you like to lead the last soul to Christ to make up His body before our Commander-in-Chief calls us all home?

CHAPTER FOURTEEN

CONCLUSION

The whole thrust of the chronological evidence presented in this book has been to alert believers and awaken unbelievers to the NEARNESS of the tribulation period. This is described by Jesus Christ as a period of ''great distress, unequalled from the beginning of the world until now - and never to be equalled again.'' (Matthew 24:21).

Dr. Leon J. Wood sums up the two main purposes of the tribulation period :-

1. Retribution on the World

One purpose is the bringing of retribution on the nations of the world for their sinfulness. All men individually have been sinners; and all nations, as collections of individuals, have likewise followed in ways not pleasing to God. The world has never witnessed the blessed existence possible on the earth, because sin has prevented the gracious benefits God has in store. One day this blessedness will be experienced, when Christ rules in justice and perfection during the millennial age. Before that time comes, however, there must be a reckoning, a time of retribution for the nations of the earth. Revelation 3:10 speaks of that time as 'the hour of temptation, which shall come upon all the world, to try them that dwell upon the earth.' In Psalm 2:5, after first telling of the continued opposition of the nations to God and His will, the psalmist states, 'Then shall He (God) speak unto them in His wrath, and vex them in His sore displeasure'. Following this, significantly, the writer refers directly to the millennial age.

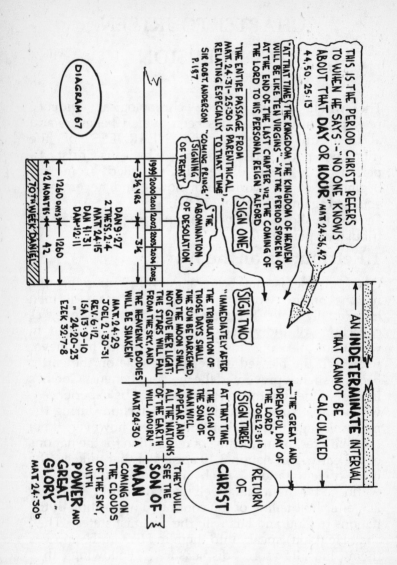

THIS IS THE PERIOD CHRIST REFERS TO WHEN HE SAYS :- "NO ONE KNOWS ABOUT THAT DAY OR HOUR" MATT 24:36,42 44,50, 25:13

"AT THAT TIME THE KINGDOM, THE KINGDOM OF HEAVEN WILL BE LIKE TEN VIRGINS"...."AT THE PERIOD SPOKEN OF AT THE END OF THE LAST CHAPTER viz THE COMING OF THE LORD TO HIS PERSONAL REIGN." ALFORD

"THE ENTIRE PASSAGE FROM MAT. 24:31-25:30 IS PARENTHICAL, RELATING ESPECIALLY TO THAT TIME."
SIR ROBT ANDERSON P.187

DIAGRAM 67

"COMING PRINCE"

"SIGNING OF TREATY"

"THE ABOMINATION OF DESOLATION"

| 1999 | 2000 | 2001 | 2002 | 2003 | 2004 | 2005 |

← 3½ YRS → ← 3½ →

DAN 9:27
2 THESS. 2:4
MAT 24:15
DAN 11:31
DAN 12:11

← 1260 DAYS → ← 1260 →
← 42 MONTHS → ← 42 →

70TH WEEK DANIEL

SIGN ONE

SIGN TWO

"IMMEDIATELY AFTER THE TRIBULATION OF THOSE DAYS SHALL THE SUN BE DARKENED, AND THE MOON SHALL NOT GIVE HER LIGHT; THE STARS WILL FALL FROM THE SKY, AND THE HEAVENLY BODIES WILL BE SHAKEN"
MAT 24:29

MAT 24:29
JOEL 2:30-31
REV: 6:12
ISA 13:9-10
" 24:20-25
EZEK 32:7-8

AN INDETERMINATE INTERVAL THAT CANNOT BE CALCULATED

"THE GREAT AND DREADFUL DAY OF THE LORD"
JOEL 2:31b

SIGN THREE

"AT THAT TIME THE SIGN OF THE SON OF MAN WILL APPEAR, AND ALL THE NATIONS OF THE EARTH WILL MOURN"
MAT 24:30 A

RETURN OF CHRIST

"THEY WILL SEE THE SON OF MAN COMING ON THE CLOUDS OF THE SKY, WITH POWER AND GREAT GLORY"
MAT 24:30b

184

2. The Time of Jacob's Trouble. (Dia.67)

The other purpose of the tribulation is the preparation of Israel to receive her Messiah. God's people must be brought to a frame of mind receptive to their Messiah. The Jews were not ready to receive Christ the first time He came, and they are not ready today. A change is needed, therefore; this change will make them ready to accept the One they have for so long rejected. However, only a major experience can bring about such a change. This is the reason for the extreme suffering of the tribulation time. Jeremiah expresses this thought in his description of the tribulation as "the time of Jacob's trouble" (30:7). Zechariah speaks of the degree of suffering involved in most sombre tones, as he states, *"And it shall come to pass, that in all the land, saith the Lord, two parts therein shall be cut off and die; but the third shall be left therein."* (13:8). Two thirds of the people will be cut off from the land, a devastation that defies full understanding, because nothing like it has ever been witnessed before. Zechariah then states the significance of this devastation, as he says, *"And I (God) will bring the third part through the fire, and will refine them as silver is refined, and will try them as gold is tried."* Finally Zechariah tells of the end accomplished by this shattering experience. *'They shall call on my name, and I will hear them: I will say, It is my people; and they shall say, 'The Lord is my God.'* (13:9). (The Bible and Future Events. p. 56-57).

So much for the bad news. Now for the good news. In the words of Josh McDowell, "The optimism portrayed by the prophets amazed me. The Bible clearly tells us that God is in control. There is hope. The world is racing towards a climax. But instead of a disastrous catastrophe, it will be Christ's dynamic return to earth to set up a thousand year reign of peace. Looking at the world situation and knowing that God is in control, I am thankful to be alive today. What an opportunity - in a time of frustration, pessimism and fear - to trust God to use His children in other people's lives; to be a ray of hope, a source of optimism, an instrument of the Holy Spirit to share Christ's love and forgiveness with others.'' (Prophecy Fact or Fiction pp 4-5) Josh McDowell.

Here is just a sample of the blessings and benefits that will accrue during the Messianic Age when Christ rules as King (Dia.68).

1. Respect and dignity for the aged and joyous safe recreation for the children.

"Thus saith the Lord of hosts, there shall yet be old men and women sit in the streets......and the streets of the city shall be full of boys and girls playing in the streets." (Zechariah 8:4-5).

2. The disappearance of physical disease and deformity

"The eyes of the blind shall be opened, and the ears of the deaf shall be unstopped. The lame man shall leap as an hart and the tongue of the dumb sing." (Isaiah 35:5-6)

3. Marriage will be restored to its pristine honour and joy

"The voice of joy, and gladness, the voice of the bridegroom and the voice of the bride shall say praise the Lord of Hosts" (Jeremiah 33:11).

Many, many more blessings are foretold by the prophets for the Messianic Age when Christ reigns supreme. But first there are breakers ahead (the tribulation) and beyond that stretch the golden shore of the Millennial Age. Soon this world will be plunged into the darkest hour before the dawn. God's message to you if you are a believer is :- *"understanding the present time. The hour has come for you to wake up from your slumber, because our salvation is nearer now than when we first believed. The night is nearly over; the day is almost here. So let us put aside the deeds of darkness and put on the armour of light."* (Romans 13:11-12).

His message to you if you are an unbeliever is clear :- *"The day of the Lord will come like a thief in the night. While*

DAY SIX	DAY SEVEN — MILLENNIUM — REST
WRATH JUDGMENT INDIGNATION TRIAL TROUBLE DESTRUCTION DARKNESS DESOLATION TRIBULATION OVERTURNING PUNISHMENT "THE DARKEST HOUR BEFORE THE DAWN"	ALL MILITARY **WARFARE** WILL BE ABOLISHED —"I WILL BREAK THE BOW AND THE SWORD AND [ABOLISH BATTLE EQUIPMENT]" HOSEA 2:18 NO MORE MILITARY **TRAINING** — NEITHER SHALL THEY LEARN WAR ANY MORE" MICAH 4:3 **MARRIAGE** WILL BE RESTORED TO ITS PRISTINE HONOR AND JOY —"THE VOICE OF JOY, AND GLADNESS, THE VOICE OF THE BRIDEGROOM, AND THE VOICE OF THE BRIDE, SHALL SAY PRAISE THE LORD OF HOSTS. JER.33:10-11.15 RESPECT AND DIGNITY FOR THE **AGED** AND JOYOUS SAFE RECREATION FOR THE **CHILDREN** —"THUS SAITH THE LORD OF HOSTS, THERE SHALL YET OLD MEN AND WOMEN SIT IN THE STREETS....AND THE STREETS OF THE CITY SHALL BE FULL OF BOYS AND GIRLS PLAYING IN THE STREETS" ZECH 8:4-5 THE **LANGUAGE** BARRIER WILL BE REMOVED —"THEN WILL I TURN TO THE PEOPLES A PURE LANGUAGE, THAT THEY MAY ALL CALL UPON THE NAME OF JEHOVAH, TO SERVE HIM WITH ONE CONSENT." ZEPH 3:9 ASV (DIA 68) DISAPPEARANCE OF PHYSICAL **DISEASE** AND **DEFORMITY** —"THE EYES THE BLIND SHALL BE OPENED, AND THE EARS OF THE DEAF SHALL BE UNSTOPPED. THE LAME MAN SHALL LEAP AS AN HART, AND THE TONGUE OF THE DUMB SING" ISA 35:5-6

people are saying 'Peace and safety,' destruction will come on them suddenly, as labour pains on a pregnant woman, and they will not escape. (1 Thessalonians 5:2-3). Even the hands of the 'Doomsday Clock' have been put back three minutes since the signing of the Nuclear Missile Treaty December 8th 1987 between the Soviet Union and U.S.A. *"This will happen when the Lord Jesus is revealed from heaven in blazing fire with His powerful angels. He will punish those who do not know God and do not obey the gospel of our Lord Jesus. They will be punished with everlasting destruction and shut out from the presence of the Lord and from the majesty of His power."* (2 Thessalonians 1:7-9).

The door of salvation for entrance into the Church, the body of Christ, is about to SHUT. When Noah entered the ark, we read *"Then the Lord shut him in,"* (Genesis 7:16). The wise virgins who were ready went in to the wedding banquet *"and the door was shut."* (Matthew 25:10).

"Later the others also came "Sir, Sir!" they said, 'Open the door for us!'

But he replied, 'I tell you the truth, I don't know you.' Therefore keep watch, because you do not know the day or the hour." (Matthew 25:11-13)

It's your choice dear reader, to be either SHUT IN or SHUT OUT!

> "One door, and only one -
> And yet its sides are two.
> Inside and outside -
> On which side are you?"

"So teach us to NUMBER our days that we may apply our hearts unto wisdom. RETURN, O Lord, how long?" (Psalm 90:12-13)

"Lord, make me to know my end, and what is the extent of my days" (Psalm 39:4)

"Be careful, or your hearts will be weighed down with dissipation, drunkenness and the anxieties of life, and that day will close on you unexpectedly like a trap. For it will come upon all those who live on the face of the whole earth. Be

always on the watch, and pray that you may be able to escape all that is about to happen and that you may be able to stand before the Son of Man.'' (Luke 21:34-35).

EPILOGUE

A LAST MINUTE CONFIRMATION

As I have been writing this book, and lecturing throughout New Zealand friends have asked, "Has anyone else found similar facts anywhere else in the world?" I have felt out on a limb because my answer has been, "not to my knowledge". But I felt sure that if these facts were true, on the basis of Matthew 18:16, *"in the mouths of two or three witnesses shall every word be established"*, some-one, elsewhere, would be picking up a similar message from the Lord.

The manuscript was about to be sent to the publisher in December 1987 when the confirming truth came from the deep heart of the United States! An old friend, Dr Dennis Spackman, gave me two tapes which described the material in a new book "Hidden Prophecies in the Psalms" by J.R.Church.*

Before outlining his major discovery, and how it unwittingly confirms the terminal year of 2005 AD, let me give you some background on the Psalms.

From Ancient Jewish times, the **LITERARY STRUCTURE** of the Psalms was known. During the nineteenth century, various writers unfolded the **PROPHETIC STRUCTURE** of the Psalms. Now, late in the twentieth century, in keeping with the doctrine of progressive illumination, the **CHRONOLOGICAL**

*Prophecy Publications, P.O. Box 7000, Oklahoma City, O.K.73153

STRUCTURE has been given to the world through "Hidden Prophecies in the Psalms."

LITERARY STRUCTURE

Ancient Jewish Authorities divided the Psalms into five books, called the "Pentateuch of David". The New International Bible has included these divisions in the Psalms. They are :-

Book One, THE GENESIS BOOK (Psalms 1-41)

Book Two, THE EXODUS BOOK (Psalms 42-72)

Book Three, THE LEVITICUS BOOK (Psalms 73-89)

Boook Four, THE NUMBERS BOOK (Psalms 90-106)

Book Five, THE DEUTERONOMY BOOK (Psalms 107-150)

For the most detailed, comprehensive charts on the structures of these five books refer to E.W.Bullinger's COMPANION BIBLE, now fortunately back in print.

PROPHETIC STRUCTURE

Nineteenth Century writers were aware that the Psalms were arranged in a prophetic sequence of events. F.W.Grant wrote in 1896, "As Old Testament prophecy, the blessing of the Psalms connects itself with the future blessing of Israel according to the New Covenant.....It will naturally follow that the Psalms cannot rightly be treated, as they too generally are, as if independent of one another, or without systematic order, or a well-defined basis of fact or doctrine.....

On the contrary, they will only be read with due intelligence when it is seen that each individual Psalm has its suited place, and organic connection with reference to the whole, and to the doctrine and prophecy of the Old Testament, nay, of the entire Word of God. The Psalms are individually much what the words in a sentence are to this, and must be studied with reference to the whole." (Numerical Bible - The Psalms p.10).

C.E. Stuart writing in 1902 said, "...the arrangement of the different Psalms in the order in which they have come down to us is not of human origin, it is the carrying out of a divine purpose." (The Psalms p.14).

CHRONOLOGICAL STRUCTURE

"Hidden Prophecies in the Psalms" was published in 1986. This book is based on the discovery that the number of each Psalm represents the equivalent year of this century, and conveys some hidden prophetic truth in relation to the Jews for the year, e.g. Psalm 17 represents 1917, when Britain's General Allenby took Jerusalem. He frightened the Turks into surrender by flying planes over the city. In verse 8 of Psalm 17 we read of "the shadow of Thy WINGS" and in verse 12 two references to a "a LION" which could symbolize Britain.

The holocaust years 1933-34 are graphically described in the equivalent Psalms, e.g. in Psalm 44 (1944) we read *"Yea, for Thy sake are we KILLED all the day long; we are counted as sheep for the slaughter."* (Psalm 44:22) Psalm 48, verse 6 refers to *"a woman in travail"*. 1948 is the year the State of Israel was born "in a day" (Isaiah 66:7-8).

On this basis Psalm 99 represents 1999, Psalm 100, 2000 AD and Psalm 105, the year 2005, our terminus ad quem! Naturally I was anxious to see if Psalm 105 truly represented our terminal year. Psalms 90-106 are THE NUMBERS BOOK, the period when in the book of Numbers God eliminated a whole generation. Entrance into the Promised Land was forfeited because of their unbelief (Numbers 14:29). Here is the STRUCTURE of the NUMBERS BOOK, from the Companion Bible, printed last century.

90-106 (p.720). THE FOURTH, OR NUMBERS
BOOK THE EARTH AND THE NATIONS
(Division, with Prologue and Epilogue.)
Prologue 90. THE REST, LOST AND NEEDED.
A   91-94. REST FOR THE EARTH DESIRED. No
hope for it will "the wicked cease from
troubling".
A   95-100. REST FOR THE EARTH
ANTICIPATED. Note the central verse of the
Psalter (96.11) and the reason (96.13).

193

A   101-105. REST FOR THE EARTH
CELEBRATED. Jehovah's throne in the
Heavens, and his Kingdom over all (103.19).
EPILOGUE 106. THE REST. HOW LOST, AND
VALUED.

Note Psalm 105 (2005 AD) is the END of this structure
and Psalm 106 is just an epilogue. Psalms 91-94 refer to
the DESIRED rest of the millennium. Psalms 95-100
ANTICIPATE the millennium, but by Psalm 105 we
have the CELEBRATION of the millennium!

   F.W. Grant in his last century 'Numerical Bible' gives
as the heading for BOOK FOUR (Psalm 90-106) "The
failed first man replaced by the second, *AND THE
WORLD ESTABLISHED under His Hand*" (emphasis
mine).

   Note the terminating PROPHETIC SEQUENCE of
these Psalms:-

104:35 *"But may sinners vanish from the earth and the
wicked be no more."*

105:7 *"His judgements are in all the earth."*

105:8-10 *"He remembers....the covenant He made with
Abraham, the oath He swore to Isaac. He confirmed it to
Jacob... as an everlasting covenant."*

105:11 *"To you I will give the land of Canaan as the portion
you will inherit."*

105:26-36 Here are detailed, the plagues God sent on
Egypt, to deliver His people from Pharaoh. In the same
way the tribulation plagues in Revelation 6-18 culminate
in Israel's deliverance. (see p.125 in the quote from Alva
McClain)

105 (2005):43-44 *"He brought out HIS people with
rejoicing, His chosen ones with shouts of joy; He gave
them the lands of the nations."*

107 (2007) Book Five opens with a marvellous hymn of
praise for Israel's deliverance.

*"Give thanks to the Lord... let the redeemed of the Lord say
this - those He redeemed from the hand of the foe, those He
gathered from the lands, from east and west, from north and
south."* (v.1-3).

They are then reminded of their trials during their dispersion *"some wandered in wastelands."* v.4 *"some sat in darkness and the deepest gloom, prisoners suffering in iron chains."* v.10 *"they loathed all foods and drew near the gates of death."* v.18 *"They reeled and staggered like drunken men; they were at their wit's end."* (v.27).

Four times we have their 'Hallelujah Chorus' of deliverance -

"Oh that men would praise the Lord for His goodness, and for His wonderful works to the children of men!" (vv.8,15,21 & 31); then the Psalm ends - *"Whoever is wise, let him heed these things and consider the great love of the Lord."* (v.43).

Thus we can see the Great Divide between Psalm 105 (2005 AD) and Psalm 107 (2007 AD). Somewhere in-between these two Psalms, Israel has crossed over into the Promised Land!

In his book, J.R. Church quoting H.A.Ironside says "The fourth book is the darkest one, for it is the book of testing, the book of trial, as in Numbers... then the last book of Psalms is the book that brings in... divine government." (p.18). Then Church says, "Yes, the fifth division of the Psalms implies the LOGOS period of world history - the millennial reign of Christ! (p.20-21). ...their Messiah will return in power and great glory to establish the Deuteronomy period of history - His millennial reign" (p.21). Again, at the end of his book he repeats "Remember, the Deuteronomy section prophetically portrays the seventh millennium of human history - the GREAT SABBATH REST wherein the Kingdom of God will be established. Psalms (95-106) give a detailed account of the judgments of Armageddon, the appearance of Christ, and the establishment of his Kingdom. They refer to a time when the Saviour will come to judge the nations, rid the world of war, reorganise the Government, remove the curse and return paradise to the planet" (p.304).

Many more aspects could be detailed, but it is abundantly clear on Church's thesis that if the Psalms in sequence represent years - then 2005 AD is the terminus ad quem!

Thus we have our three witnesses to the year 2005 AD

1. 1961 "The Times of the Gentiles" A.E.Bloomfield. Refer back to p.37.
2. 1986 "Hidden Prophecies in the Psalms" J.R.Church
3. 1988 The many bearings in this book.

From then on *"the government shall be upon His shoulder."* (Isaiah 9:6)

"The Lord will be King over the whole earth. On that day there will be one Lord, and His name the only name." (Zechariah 14:19)

"What I have said, that will I bring about; what I have planned, that will I do. Listen to me you stubborn-hearted, you who are far from righteousness. I am bringing My righteousness near, IT IS NOT FAR AWAY: and My Salvation WILL NOT BE DELAYED. I will grant salvation to Zion, My Splendour to Israel.": (Isaiah 46:11-13)

Praise the Lord,
Praise God in His Sanctuary;
Praise Him in His Mighty Heavens....
Let everything that has breath praise the Lord.
Praise the Lord. (Psalm 150)

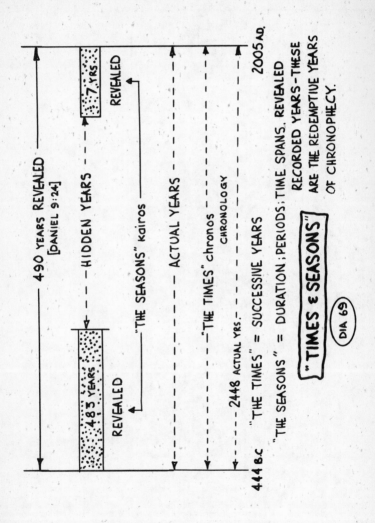

490 YEARS REVEALED
[DANIEL 9:24]

--- HIDDEN YEARS ---

7 YRS.

REVEALED

483 YEARS

REVEALED

"THE SEASONS" kairos

----- ACTUAL YEARS -----

-- "THE TIMES" chronos --
CHRONOLOGY

--- 2448 ACTUAL YRS. ---

444 B.C.   2005 A.D.

"THE TIMES" = SUCCESSIVE YEARS

"THE SEASONS" = DURATION; PERIODS; TIME SPANS. REVEALED
RECORDED YEARS — THESE
ARE THE REDEMPTIVE YEARS
OF CHRONOPHECY.

"TIMES & SEASONS"

DIA 69

197

APPENDIX 1

In Bible chronophecy it is important to know your three 'R's' - and to distinguish between them.

1. REAL or actual years based on the solar year of 365.24 days.
2. REVEALED or RECORDED years as based on the biblical data - most are solar years but some as in Daniel's 70 weeks (Daniel 9) are of 360 days. (Dia. 69).
3. REDEMPTIVE years. Not all the revealed years are reckoned in Bible chronophecy, because time did not count with God when His people (Israel) were out of fellowship with Him. (See Chronology of the Old Testament, Martin Anstey p.p.79-80).

This whole work has been based on the RECKONABLE years of redemptive chronology as revealed in the Scriptures - not on the REAL years one would use in computing the chronology of the world.

Dr. Green's valuable explanation of the Bible genealogies is included in the book 'Evolution' by Pattle Pun (p.p.256-260) as follows:

GENEALOGIES OF THE BIBLE

Dr. W.H. Green, late professor of Old Testament at Princeton Theological Seminary and a contributor to the famous Fundamentals papers, has succinctly analyzed the genealogies of the Bible. He concluded that they were not intended and cannot be legitimately used to construct a chronology. His conclusions have been collaborated by other biblical scholars. The arguments against the chronological treatment of the biblical genealogies can be summarized in the following three points:

1. Abridgment and omission of unimportant names is the pattern in the genealogies of the Bible. There are numerous examples of this observation. One prime example is the omissions in the genealogies of the Lord Jesus. In Matthew 1:8 Ahaziah (2 Kings 8:25), Joash (2 Kings 7:1), and Amaziah (2 Kings 23:34; 1 Chronicles 3:16) are dropped between Joram and Ozias (or Uzziah). In Matthew 1:1 the entire genealogy of Jesus is summed up in two steps, ''Jesus Christ the son of David, the son of Abraham.''

A comparison of 1 Chronicles 6:3-14 and Ezra 7:1-5 also reveals that six consecutive names in the genealogy of Ezra were omitted in the book that bears his name. The genealogy in Exodus 6:16-25 makes Moses the great-grandson of Levi though 430 years intervened (Exodus 12.40). It is, therefore, evident that many names have been omitted from Moses' genealogy.

Another convincing proof is found in Numbers 3:19, 27-28. Four sons of Kohath, or grandsons of Levi, appear respectively to give rise to the families of the Amramites, Izharites, Hebronites, and Uzzielites. The number of males in these families one month and upward was 8600 only one year after the Exodus. It is inconceivable to assume that the father of Moses had given birth to 8600 descendants of the male sex alone, and 2750 of them were between the ages of 30 and 50 (Numbers 4;36).

2. Genealogies include significant names. Biblical writers did not have chronology in mind when they wrote the genealogies. The genealogy of our Lord Jesus in Matthew 1 covered three lists of 14 generations. Each list covered different lengths of time, according to archaeological findings: Abraham to David nearly 1000 years, David to the Exile about 400 years, and the Exile to Christ more than 500 years. In verse 6 David is counted as the last of 14 generations extending from Abraham through David. David is also counted again as the first of 14 generations extending from David to the Exile. Therefore, David is counted twice in the genealogical record.

At the same time, the four women listed in the genealogy of Jesus — Tamar (v.3), Rahab (v.5), Ruth (v.5), and the wife of Uriah (v.6) - were not counted in Matthew's final tabulation of generations. The listing of these women in the genealogy was contrary to the Jewish custom. Yet each of these women was remarkable in some way. Three were once guilty of gross sin (Tamar, Rahab, and the wife of Uriah), and Ruth was of Gentile origin. This circumstance seems to indicate that Matthew did not simply copy the genealogical history of Joseph. He seemed to have a specific purpose in mind, and he omitted what did not suit the purpose or added what did.

The genealogies in Genesis 5 and 11 pertain to the generations elapsed from Adam to the Flood and from the Flood to Abraham, respectively. There is no passage in the Bible specifying the total length of time that actually transpired from Adam to the Flood and from the Flood to Abraham. However, some dates after the Flood-to-Abraham period are given - the period from Joseph to Moses was recorded as 430 years (Exodus 12:40), and the time elapsed from the Exodus to the building of the temple was 480 years (1 Kings 6:1). The absence of recorded elapsed time from Adam to Abraham suggests that this was an indefinite period of time on which Moses was not given exact information by God.

The stuctures of the genealogies in Genesis 5 and 11 seem to be symmetrical. Each genealogy includes 10 names; Noah is 10 persons from Adam, and Terah is 10 persons from Noah. Each ends with a father having three sons, and the Cainite genealogy (Genesis 4:17-22) ends this way also. The Cainite and Sethite genealogies terms of Lemech's polygamy, bloody revenge, and boastful arrogance, and Enoch's godliness and direct ascent to God, respectively.

The absence of accurately recorded time from Adam to Abraham and the symmetrical structures of the genealogies in Genesis 5 and 11 are highly suggestive of intentional arrangement in a form similar to that of Matthew. If one assumes that a long period of time elapsed between Adam and Abraham, the meager biblical record of events that transpired during this period is not suprising, for it is not uncommon for Scripture to pass over long periods of time with little or no remark. For example, the greater part of the 430 years of the sojourn of the Israelites in Egypt is left blank in the sacred history.

3. "Father," "son", and "begot" were used in a broad sense. Several Biblical passages contain ancestral titles used in a broad sense. We know from earlier discussion that several names have been omitted in Matthew 1:8 after Joram. Therefore, Joram was actually the great-great grandfather of Uzziah. It is obvious that the "father" used in verse 8 between Joram and Uzziah means "ancestor" instead if its conventional meaning. In 1 Chronicles 1:36 the Hebrew text includes seven names after "the sons of Eliphaz," making it appear that all the seven named are sons. Actually one of the names, Timna, was that of a concubine, not a son. Only the New International Version translates clearly that Timna was Eliphaz's concubine, as recorded also in Genesis 36:11-12, and the other six are sons.

The genealogy of Samuel in 1 Chronicles 6:22-24, 37-38 suggests that an individual is a son of the preceding descendant: "The descendants Kohath: Amminadab his son, Korah his son, Assir his son, Elkanah his son, Ebiasaph his son, Assir his son" (v.22-23 NIV). However, the first Assir, Eklanah, and Ebiasaph were all sons of Korah and thus brothers. Korah's father, Amminadab is also called Izhar in verse 38. This practice of listing dual names is common throughout the Bible.

Matthew 1:1 reads." Jesus Christ the son of David, the son of Abraham." "Son" here obviously means descendant. Therefore, the biblical writers and translators seem to use the words "father" and "son" freely to mean "ancestor" or "descendant", and sometimes the persons are not closely related.

The regular formula in the genealogies in Genesis 5 and 10 is "A lived — years and begat B, and A lived after he begat B — years and begat sons and daughters. And B lived — years and begat C......" (KJV). The Hebrew word "begat" is sometimes used for succeeding generations. Zilpah is said to have "born to" Jacob her great-grandchildren (Genesis 46:18 NIV) and Bilhah her grandchildren (Genesis 46:25). Canaan is recorded to have begotten whole nations (Genesis 10:15-18).

Furthermore, if the dates are true, Adam was contemporary with every generation until the Flood, except Noah. Methuselah died in the year of the Flood. Shem survived Abraham for 35 years; Salah, 3 years; and Eber, 64 years. For 58 years Noah was the contemporary of Abraham, and Shem actually survived Abraham for 35 years. Such conclusions are contrary to the spirit of the record that presupposed a much longer gap between Noah and Abraham.

A comparison of the Hebrew text with the Septuagint (Greek) and the Samaritan Pentateuch also reveals discrepancies in the years assigned to the antidiluvial patriarchs. Different versions seek to bring the ages of the patriarchs into closer conformity. The Samaritan and the Septuagint versions vary systematically from the Hebrew text, suggesting that these translations were trying to accommodate the Mosaic narratives to the demands of the accepted Egyptian antiquity at the time. However, the Hebrew text (AD 980), although it came much later than the Septuagint (250-150 BC) and the Samaritan Pentateuch (143-37 BC), was well established as the most accurate, original transcript of the Old Testament.

Moses, who lived for some time in Egypt, must have known as much about the age of Egypt as the Septuagint translators or any other translators. If some translators felt that the original genealogy from which they drew their infomation was inadmissible to fit the antiquity of Egypt, and that they had to introduce up to 900 years into the lives of the patriarch, it is highly suggestive that Moses did not intend for the genealogies to be interpreted chronologically. This suggestion was born out by the inclusion of Cainan (Luke 3:36) in the genealogy of Jesus. This name was not found in the Hebrew text, but it occurs in Genesis 11:13 in the Septuagint Old Testament.

W.H. Green concluded his paper with the following statement: "On these various grounds we conclude that the Scriptures furnish no data for a chronological computation prior to the life of Abraham, and that the Mosaic records do not fix and were not intended to fix the precise date either of the Flood or of the creation of the world."

Thus the purpose of the genealogies in Genesis 5 and 11 seems to be more to show the effect of sin on human vitality and longevity rather than to establish chronology. In the formula discussed above, B could be the literal son of a distant descendant, and the age of A may be his age at the birth of the child from whom B was descended. This may allow centuries, millenniums, or hundreds of thousands of years to intervene between A and B.

The proponents of a recent creation have revised their date of creation back to 10,000 BC or so because of these arguments. However, they will not make any further concession, for this would introduce too large a gap into the genealogies. However, it is entirely personal preference and not based on any exegetical data.

Bible passages referring to "the last days (times)" (Matthew 28:20; Acts 2:17; Hebrews 1:2; 9:26; 1 Peter 1:20; 1 John 2:18) and the promise of Jesus' imminent return (Revelation 1:3; 22:10; 12:20) fit in nicely with the assumption that humans have existed for hundreds of thousands of years prior to Christ's first coming. The use of "last days" implies that the major part of the world's history has been finished. The passages indicate that Christ's coming is to be expected within a short period, yet over 2000 years have passed since the promises. When contrasted with the thousands of years people have existed on earth, it is a short time. However, the passages are far-fetched if it is assumed

204

that created life has existed for only 4000 - 10,000 years, because one would be forced to interpret the "last days" to mean the last one-half to one-fifth of the created order. This assumption seems to misread the intent of the "last days" passages.

APPENDIX 2

(Dia.70)
THE SEVENTY WEEKS OF DANIEL

The classic book on this subject is 'The Coming Prince'' by Sir Robert Anderson. A simpler condensed book is "Daniel's Prophecy of the Seventy Weeks" by Alva McClain - both these books have been updated in the light of recent research by Harold W. Hoehner, "Chronological Aspects of the Life of Christ." This updated material is well presented in Josh McDowell's excellent book "Prophecy Fact or Fiction."

The following is the footnote to Daniel 9:24-27 in the new Scofield Bible.

"Daniel's prophecy of the seventy 'sevens' (weeks) (vv. 24-27) provides the chronological frame for Messianic prediction from Daniel to the establishment of the kingdom on earth and also a key to its interpretation. Its main features are as follows:

1. The entire prophecy is concerned primarily with Daniel's "people" and the "holy city" - i.e. Israel and Jerusalem.
2. Two princes are mentioned; the first is named "the Anointed One, the ruler" (i.e. Messiah, the Prince) (v.25); the second is described as "the ruler who will come" (v.26), a reference to the little horn of ch. 7:8, whose "people" would destroy the rebuilt Jerusalem after the cutting off of the Messianic Prince (v.26).
3. The "seventy sevens" of the prophecy are weeks of years, an important sabbatical time-measure in the Jewish calendar. Violation of the command to observe the sabbatical year brought the judgment of the Babylonian captivity and determined its length of

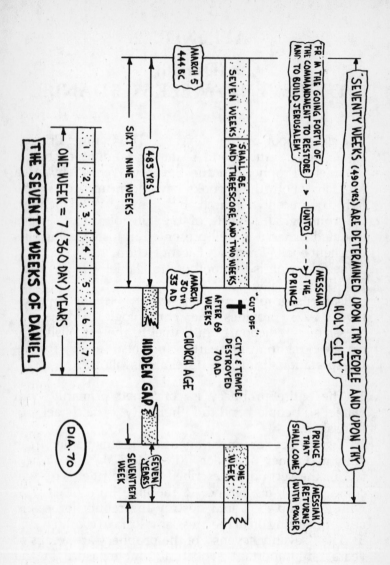

THE SEVENTY WEEKS OF DANIEL

ONE WEEK = 7 (360 DAY) YEARS

| 1 | 2 | 3 | 4 | 5 | 6 | 7 |

DIA. 70

SEVENTY WEEKS (490 YRS) ARE DETERMINED UPON THY PEOPLE AND UPON THY HOLY CITY

FR'M THE GOING FORTH OF THE COMMANDMENT TO RESTORE AND TO BUILD JERUSALEM

UNTO

MESSIAH THE PRINCE

MARCH 5 444 BC

SEVEN WEEKS

SHALL BE AND THREESCORE AND TWO WEEKS

SIXTY NINE WEEKS

483 YRS

MARCH 30TH 33 AD

AFTER 69 WEEKS

"CUT OFF"

CITY & TEMPLE DESTROYED 70 AD

CHURCH AGE

HIDDEN GAP

PRINCE THAT SHALL COME

MESSIAH RETURNS WITH POWER

SEVENTIETH WEEK

SEVEN YEARS

ONE WEEK

208

seventy years. Compare Leviticus 25:1-22, 26:33-35; 2 Chronicles 36:19-21; Daniel 9:2. Compare also Genesis 29:26-28 for use of "week" to indicate seven years.

4. These 490 prophetic years are each 360 days long. This is proved by the Biblical references to the seventieth week of seven years, which is divided into two halves (v.27), the latter half being various designated as "a time, times, and half a time" (Daniel 7:25; cp Revelation 12:14); forty-two months (Revelation 11:2; 13:5); or 1260 days (Revelation 11:3; 12:6). In this connection it should be remembered that, in the grand sweep of prophecy, prophetic time is invariably so near as to give full warning, so indeterminate as to give no satisfaction to mere curiosity (cf. Matthew 24:36; Acts 1:7).

5. The beginning of the seventy weeks is fixed as "the issuing of the decree to restore and rebuild Jerusalem" and its wall (v.25). The only decree in Scripture authorizing the rebuilding of the city and its wall is recorded in Nehemiah 2; dated in "the month of Nisan in the twentieth year of King Artaxerxes" (i.e. 444 B.C.), it is well attested in ancient history. From this date as a beginning, the first sixty-nine weeks reach to "the Anointed One, the ruler."

6. At a later time, after the "sixty-two 'sevens'" which follow the first "seven weeks" i.e. after sixty-nine weeks), two important events will take place: (1) Messiah will be "cut off' and will have none of His regal rights ("will have nothing"). And (2) the rebuilt city and sanctuary will again be destroyed, this time by "the people of another "ruler" who is yet to come. It is generally agreed that these two events were fulfilled in the death of Christ (33 AD.) and the destruction of Jerusalem by Rome in AD. 70. Both events are placed before the seventieth week of v.27. Hence a period of at least thirty-seven years between the death of Christ and the destruction of Jerusalem must intervene between the sixty-ninth and seventieth weeks.

7. The main events of the final "one 'seven'" (v.27 are as follows: (1) There is a seven-year "covenant" made

by the future Roman prince (the "little horn" of 7:8) with the Jews. (2) In the middle of the week there is a forcible interruption of the Jewish ritual of workship by the Roman prince who intoduces "abomination" that renders the sanctuary desolate. (3) At the same time he launches persecution against the Jews. And (4) the end of the seventieth week brings judgment upon the desolator and also brings "everlasting righteousness" (v.24 - i.e. the blessings of the Messianic Kingdom.)

The proof that his final week has not yet been fulfilled is seen in the fact that Christ definitely relates its main events to His second coming (Matthew 24:6,15). Hence, during the interim between the sixty-ninth and seventieth weeks there must lie the whole period of the Church set forth in the N.T. but not revealed in the O.T.

The interpretation which assigns the last of the seventy weeks to the end of the age is found in the Church Fathers. When this seventieth week was referred to during the first two and one-half centuries of the Christian Church, it was almost always assigned to the end of the age. Irenaeus places the appearance of Antichrist at the end of the age in the last week; in fact, he asserts that the time of Antichrist's tyranny will last just one-half of the week, three years and six months. So likewise Hippolytus states that Daniel "indicates the showing forth of the seven years which shall be in the last times."

Note 1

The two dates 445 BC and 32 AD in this article have been updated in the light of the latest scholarship to 444 BC and 33 AD. Refer 'Chronological Aspects of the Life of Christ' Harold W. Hoehner.

Note 2

Throughout this book, dates back to the Exodus have been based on the data in 'The Mysterious Numbers of the Hebrew Kings' Thiele; in conjunction of course with the Biblical text.

Dates prior to the Exodus are based entirely on the biblical chronology. The time spans (not the dates) are those of Archbishop Ussher and the Rev. Martin Anstey. (Dia. 72)

KEY DATES OF REDEMPTIVE CHRONOLOGY

1951 BC Birth of Abram
1941 BC Birth of Sarah
1851 BC Birth of Isaac
1846 BC Weaning of Isaac
1791 BC Birth of Jacob
1700 BC Birth of Joseph
1526 BC Birth of Moses
1446 BC The Exodus
1010 BC David crowned King
1002 BC David captures Jerusalem
966 BC Solomon's Temple commenced
930/31 BC Death of Solomon & Division of the Kingdom
586 BC Destruction of Jerusalem & Temple
516 BC Completion of Second Temple
444 BC Edict to rebuild Jerusalem
33 AD The Death of Jesus Christ

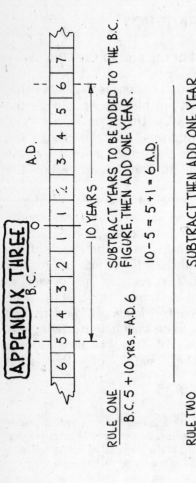

APPENDIX THREE

B.C. ――――――――――――― A.D.

| 6 | 5 | 4 | 3 | 2 | 1 | 0 | 1 | 2 | 3 | 4 | 5 | 6 | 7 |

10 YEARS

RULE ONE
B.C. 5 + 10 YRS. = A.D. 6

SUBTRACT YEARS TO BE ADDED TO THE B.C. FIGURE, THEN ADD ONE YEAR.

10 − 5 = 5 + 1 = 6 A.D.

RULE TWO
A.D. 6 − 10 YRS = B.C. 5

SUBTRACT, THEN ADD ONE YEAR.

10 − 6 = 4 + 1 = 5 B.C.

RULE THREE
B.C. 5 TO A.D. 6 = 10 YRS.

ADD B.C. YEARS TO A.D. YEARS, THEN SUBTRACT ONE.

B.C. 5 + A.D. 6 = 11 − 1 = 10 YRS.

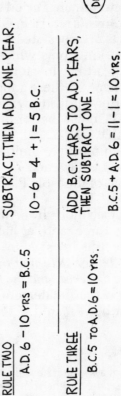
(DIA. 71)

CALCULATING ACROSS B.C. TO A.D. YEARS

213

APPENDIX 4

The Indeterminate Period at the end of the 70th Week prior to Christ's return in Glory.

And it is expressly stated * that his rise is to be *after* that of the ten kingdoms which are hereafter to divide the Roman earth. It follows, therefore, that the development of these kingdoms, and the rise of the great Kaiser who is to wield the imperial sceptre in the last days, must be prior to the beginning of the seventieth week.

And within certain limits, we can also fix the order of the subsequent events. The violation of the treaty by the defilement of the Holy Place is to occur "in the midst of the week." That even, again, is to be the epoch of the great persecution by Antichrist,§ which is to last precisely three and a half years; for his power to persecute the Jews is to be limited to that definite period. *"Immediately after the tribulation of those days shall the sun be darkened, and the moon shall not give her light."* Such is the statement of the twenty fourth of Matthew, and the sixth of Revelation

★ ★ ★

* Dan.7:24

+ I do not assert that he will have reached the zenith of his power before that date. On the contrary, it seems extremely probable that the treaty with the Jews will be one of the steps by which he will raise himself to the place he is destined to hold, and that as soon as he has attained his end, he will throw off the mask and declare himself a persecutor. So Irenaeus teaches, and he possibly gives what was the tradition of the apostolic age.

§ Dan.9:27   § Matt.14:15-21
  Dan.7:25;Rev.8:5.   Matt.14:29

exactly coincides with it, for the vision of the fifth seal embraced the period of *"the tribulation"*; and when the sixth seal was opened, *"the sun became black as sackcloth of hair, and the moon became as blood,"* and the cry went forth, *"The great day of His wrath is come."* In keeping with this, again, is the prophecy of Joel: *"The sun shall be turned into darkness, and the moon into blood, before the great and the terrible day of the Lord come."* + The events of this day of vengeance are the burden of the vision of the seventh seal, including the judgment of Babylon, the scarlet woman-or the religious apostasy-by the agency of the imperial power -but the beast, whose fearful end is to bring the awful drama to a close.§

We have definite grounds, therefore, for assigning the following order to the events of the last days:-

1. The development of the ten kingdoms.

2. The appearance within the territorial limits of these kingdoms of an eleventh "king", who will subdue three of the ten, and will ultimately be accepted as Suzerain by all.

3. The making of a treaty by this king with, or in favour of, the Jews. *The epoch of the seventieth week.*

4. The violation of the treaty by this king after three and a half years.

5. "The great tribulation" of Scripture, the awful persecution of the last days, which shall continue three and a half years.

6. The deliverance of the Jews from their great enemy, to be followed by their final establishment in blessing. *The close of the seventieth week.*

7. "The great and terrible day of the Lord," the period of the seventh seal, beginning with a revelation of Christ to His people in Jerusalem, accompanied by appalling manifestations of Divine power and ending with His last glorious advent.

★　★　★

Rev.6:12,17   Joel 2:31
Rev.17:16,17   § Rev.19:20

That the seventieth week will be the last seven years of the dispensation, and the term of the reign of Antichrist, is a belief as old as the writings of the Ante-Nicene Fathers. But a careful examination of the statements of Scripture will lead to some modification of this view. The fulfilment to Judah of the blessings specified in Daniel 9:24 is all that Scripture expressly states will mark the close of the seventieth week. Antichrist will then be driven out of Judea; but there is no reason whatever to suppose he will otherwise lose his power. As already shown, the seventieth week ends with the period of the fifth seal, whereas the fall of Babylon is within the era of the seventh seal. No one may assert that that era will be of long duration, and it will probably be brief; but the only certain indication of its length is that it will be within a single lifetime, for at its close the Antichrist is to be seized alive, and hurled to his awful doom.*

The analogy of the past might lead us to expect that the events foretold to occur at the end of the seventieth week would follow immediately at its close. But the Book of Daniel expressly teaches that there will be an interval. Whatever view be taken of the earlier portion of the eleventh of Daniel, it is clear that "the king" of the thirty-sixth and following verses is the great enemy of the last days. His wars and conquests are predicted, and the twelfth chapter opens with the mention of the predicted time of trouble, "the great tribulation" of Matthew and Revelation. The seventh verse specifies the duration of the "time of trouble" as "a time, times, and a half," which, as already shown,   is the half week, or 1,260 days. But the eleventh verse expressly declares

★ ★ ★

* Rev.19:20

+ He is neither king of the north nor of the south, for both these kings shall invade his territory (ver.40) *i.e.,* the powers which shall then respectively possess Syria and Egypt .

See p.73, *ante.*

that from the date of the event which is to divide the week, and which, according to Matthew xxiv., is to be the signal of persecution, there shall be 1,290 days; and the twelfth verse postpones the blesing to 1,335 days, or seventy-five days beyond the close of the prophetic weeks.

If, therefore, "the day of the Lord" follows immediately upon the close of the seventieth week, it seems that Judah's complete deliverance is not to take place until after that final period has begun. And this is expressly confirmed by the fourteenth chapter of Zechariah. It is a prophecy than which none is more definite, and the difficulties which beset the interpretation of it are in no degree overcome by refusing to read it literally. It seems to teach that at that time Jerusalem is to be taken by the allied armies of the nations, and that at the moment when a host of prisoners are being led away, God will intervene in some miraculous way, as when He destroyed the army of Pharaoh at the Exodus.*

Comparison with the prophecy of the twenty-fourth chapter of St. Matthew is the surest and strictest test which can be applied to these conclusions. After fixing the epoch and describing the character of the great persecution of the last days, the Lord thus enumerates the events which are to follow at its close:*-First the great natural phenomena predicted; then the

★ ★ ★

* "The day of battle (Zechariah 14:3). The prophet adds: "And His feet shall stand on that day upon the Mount of Olives." I cannot conceive how any one can suppose this to be the great and final advent in glory as described in Matthew 24:30 and other Scriptures.

"The prophecy (Zechariah 14) seems literal. If Antichrist be the leader of the nations, it seems inconsistent with the statement that he will at this time be sitting in the temple as God at Jerusalem; thus Antichrist outside would be made to besiege Antichrist within the city. But difficulties do not set aside revelations; the event will clear up seeming difficulties" (Fausset's Commentary, in loco). It is idle to speculate on such a matter, but I presume the city will have revolted against the great enemy during his absence at the head of the armies

appearance of the sign of the Son of man in heaven; then the mourning of the tribes of the land; and finally the glorious advent.

That there will be *no* interval between the persecution and the "great signs from heaven"* which are to follow it, is expressly stated; they are to occur *"immediately after the tribulation."* That an interval shall separate the other events of the series is equally clear. From the defilement of the Holy Place, to the day when the tribulation shall end, and the "fearful sights" and "great signs" from heaven shall strike terror into men's hearts, shall be a definite period of 1,260 days; and yet when He goes to speak of the Advent, the Lord declares that that day is known to the Father only: it should be His people's part to watch and wait. He had already warned them against being deceived by expecting His Advent before the fulfilment of all that must come to pass. Now He warns them against apostasy after the accomplishment of all things, because of the delay which even then shall still mark His coming.§

The words of Christ are unequivocally true, and He never enjoins upon His people to live in expectation of His coming, save at a time when nothing intervenes to

of the empire, and that thereupon he will turn back to reconquer it. History repeats itself. Moreover, there is no reason to believe that he will reside in Jerusalem, though presumably he will have a palace there, and as part of a blasphemous pageant, will sit enthroned in the temple. That Jerusalem should be captered by a hostile army at such a time will seem less strange if it be remembered first that the true people of God therein shall have warning to leave the city at the beginning of these troubles (Matthew 24:15,16), and secondly that the deliverance of the capital is to be the last act in the deliverance of Judah (See Zechariah 12:7).

* *"Immediately after the tribulation of those days shall the sun be darkened, and the moon shall not give her light, and the stars shall fall from heaven, and the powers of the heavens shall be shaken: and then shall appear the sign of the Son of man in heaven; and then shall all the tribes of the earth mourn, and they shall see the Son of man coming in the clouds of heaven, with power and great glory"* (Matthew 24:29,30 Comp.Zech.12:12 (LXX)).

bar the fulfilment of the hope. Fatalism is as popular among Christians as with the worshippers of Mahomet; and it is forgotten that though the dispensation has run its course these eighteen centuries, it might have been brought to a close at any moment. Hence the Christian is taught to live *"looking for that blessed hope."* It will be otherwise in days to come, when the present dispensation shall have closed with the first stage of the Advent. Then the word will be, not, *"Watch, for ye know not what hour your Lord doth come,"* - that belongs to the time when all shall have been fulfilled,-but *"Take heed that no man deceive you, all these things must come to pass, but the end is not yet."*

Therefore if the Advent synchronized with these events, anyone then living would be able to fix the date of it, once the epoch of the tribulation were known; whereas the chapter clearly shows that an interval will follow after all has been fulfilled, long enough to weed out mere professors, who, tired of waiting, will apostatize (Matthew 24:48), and to lull even true disciples to a sleep from which their Lord's return will rouse them. (Ibid.25:5).

§ *Matthew 24:42-51, and 25:1-13:* "THEN shall the kingdom of heaven be likened unto ten virgins ." Though applicable to every age in which there is a waiting people on earth, the parable will have its full and special application in the last days to those who shall be looking back on the complete page of prophecy fulfilled. The entire passage from chap. 24:31, to chap. 25:30, is parenthetical, relating especialy to that time.

Titus 2:12,13.   Matthew 24:42.

From Sir Robert Anderson's Book 'The Coming Prince' (pp.182-189) 13th Edition

RECOMMENDED BOOKS ON THE RAPTURE

'THE RAPTURE' SCHUYLER ENGLISH
                    LOIZEAUX BROS   1954
'THE RAPTURE QUESTION' WALVOORD
                    DUNHAM PUB.   1957
'THE PRETRIBULATION RAPTURE' BEECHICK
                    ACCENT PUB.   1980
'THE RAPTURE' RYRIE MOODY PRESS   1981
'THE RAPTURE' HAL LINDSEY
                    BANTAM BOOKS   1983
'THE RAPTURE - PRE, MID, OR POST
TRIBULATIONAL?'   ACADEMIC BOOKS   1984

SELECT BIBLIOGRAPHY

Sir Robert Anderson	'The Coming Prince'	Pickering and Inglis 1909
Sir Robert Anderson	'Forgotten Truths'	Undated
Anglican Speakers	Commentary	John Murray 1871
Martin Anstey	'Chronology of the old Test.'	Kregel 1913
David Baron	'Israel in the Plan of God'	Kregel 1925
Rev.M.Baxter	'Louis Napoleon Destined Monarch of the World'	A.J.Smith 1866
Charles Berlitz	'Doomsday 1999'	Souvenir Press 1981
Arthur Bloomfield	'The End of the Days'	Bethany Fellowship 1961
E.W.Bullinger	'Companion Bible'	Oxford University Press Undated
E.W.Bullinger	'Number in Scripture'	Kregel 1892
E.W.Bullinger	'The Witness of the Stars'	Kregel 1893
Harry Bultman	'Maranatha'	Kregel 1985
L.E.Chafer	'Systematic Theology'	Dallas Seminary Press 1948
Maxwell Coder	'Jude'	Moody Press 1958
Joan Coman	'The Temple of Jerusalem'	Weidenfeld and Nicholson 1975
L.R.Conradi	'The Impelling Force of Prophetic Truth'	Thynne & Co. Ltd. 1935

Robert Culver	'Daniel and the Latter Days'	Moody Press 1954
J.N.Darby	'Lectures on the Second Coming'	G.Morrish 1909
Max.I.Dimont	'Jews, God and History'	Signet 1962
Abba Eban	'Heritage, Civilization and the Jews'	Weidenfeld and Nicholson 1984
E.Schuyler English	'The Rapture'	Loizeaus Bros. 1954
H.G.B.Erickstad	'Prophecies of Nostradamus'	Vantage Press 1982
Charles Lee Feinberg	'The Prophecies of Ezekiel'	Moody Press 1969
Edward Gibbon	'Decline & Fall Roman Empire'	Everyman's Library 1910
F.W.Grant	'The Numerical Bible'	Loizeaus Bros. 1891
H.Grattan Guiness	'Light for the Last Days'	Hodder & Stoughton 1886
Harold W.Hoehner	'Chronological Aspects Life of Christ'	Zondervan 1977
Stephen Howarth	'The Knights Templar'	Atheneum 1982
William L.Hull	'The Rise and Fall of Israel'	Zondervan 1954
Dave Hunt	'Beyond Seduction'	Harvest House 1987
H.A.Ironside	'The Mystery in Daniel's Prophecy'	Zondervan 1943
Arthur W.Kac	'Rebirth State of Israel'	Marshall, Morgan & Scott 1958
Harry Lacey	'God and the Nations'	John Ritchie 1942

Lance Lambert	'Till the Day Dawns'	Kingsway Publications 1982
Jerry Landay	'Dome of the Rock'	Newsweek 1972
Bob Leaman	'Armageddon'	Greenhouse Publications 1986
Hal Lindsey	'The Rapture'	Bantam Books 1983
John D.Levenson	'Sinai and Zion'	Winston Press 1985
Thomas S.McCall & Zola Levitt	'Satan in the Sanctuary'	Moody Press 1973
Alva McClain	'The Greatness of the Kingdom'	Zondervan 1959
Alva McClain	Daniel's Prophecy of the 70 Weeks'	Zondervan 1940
Josh McDowell	'Prophecy Fact or Fiction'	Campus Crusade 1979
J.Eustace Mills	'Sabbatical Typology'	The Lamp Press Ltd. Not dated.
E.J.Pace	'The Law of the Octave'	Bible Inst. Colportage Assn. 1922
J.Dwight Pentecost	'Things to Come'	Dunham Publishing Co. 1958
John Pimplot	'The Middle East Conflicts'	Orbis Publishing 1983
Walter K.Price	'The Coming Antichrist'	Loizeaus Bros. 1974
Derek Prince	'Last Word on the Middle East'	Kingsway Publications 1982
Pattle P.T.Pun	'Evolution	Zondervan 1982
James Reid	'God, The Atom and the Universe'	Zondervan 1968

223

G.B.Stanton	'Kept from the Hour'	Zondervan 1956
C.E.Stuart	'The Book of Praises'	E.Marlborough & Co. 1902
Frank H.Stuckert	'August 1999'	Exposition Press 1978
Edwin R.Thiele	'The Mysterious Numbers of the Hebrew Kings'	Paternoster Press 1951
Paul Lee Tan	'The Interpretation of Prophecy'	Cushing Malloy Inc. 1974
W.Trotter	'Plain Papers on Prophetic Subjects'	G.Morrish Undated 19th Century
John F.Walvord	'Daniel'	Moody Press 1971
John F.Walvord	'The Rapture Question'	Dunham Publications 1957
John F.Walvord	'The Revelation of Jesus Christ'	Marshall, Morgan & Scott. 1966
Max Wurmbrandt & Cecil Roth	'The Jewish People'	Cassel London 1966
Leon Wood	'A Survey of Israel's History'	Zondervan 1970
Leon Wood	'The Bible and Future Events'	Academic Books 1973

Terminus Ad Quem!!